CW00551085

SOCIAL INNOVATION IN IRELAND: CHALLENGES AND PROSPECTS

Edited by
Ronaldo Munck, Deiric Ó Broin and Jordana Corrigan

GLASNEVIN
PUBLISHING

Published in 2017 by

Glasnevin Publishing
2nd Floor, 13 Upper Baggot Street
Dublin 4, Ireland
www.glasnevinpublishing.com

Papers used by Glasnevin Publishing are from well managed forests and other responsible sources.

ISBN: 978-1-908689-33-7

Contents

LIST OF FIGURES

LIST OF TABLES

ACKNOWLEDGEMENTS

This book is the result of our discussions and contact with many people at various places over the course of the past year. The editors would like to thank those that attended the inaugural Social Innovation: Lagan to Liffey conference which took place on the 2nd November 2016 at the Dundalk Institute of Technology which marked the launch of the North-South Social Innovation Network.

The editors would like to thank the representatives that form the Steering Committee of the North South Social Network; Dublin City University, Ulster University, Dundalk Institute of Technology, The Centre for Cross Border Studies, The Wheel, Innovation Probation Board NI, Probation Service, Queens University Belfast, Fab Foundation Ireland, Creative Spark, Northern Ireland Council for Voluntary Action, Institute of Technology Blanchardstown and The Young Foundation

Deiric would like to acknowledge the many interesting, provocative, and at times zealous discussions with his colleagues in the North Dublin Political Economy Discussion Group. He would also like to thank colleagues in Pobal, Dublin City Council's Social Enterprise Committee and the Irish Social Enterprise Network. Finally, the staff of the Dublin City Library in Cabra were amazing and their colleague, Conor Darcy, who recently passed away, made the library a second home despite all the odd book requests.

Jordana would like to thank the contributors for their valuable and varying perspectives, and those that gave their time generously to discuss the themes contained within this book. She would like to thank Lisa O'Quinn for sharing her experiences and views of social innovation from a US perspective so enthusiastically over early morning Facebook calls, and Deiric Ó Broin and Ronaldo Munck for their advice and guidance.

CONTRIBUTORS

Rodd Bond is director of NetwellCASALA, the centre for ageing research, within the School of Health and Sciences at Dundalk Institute of Technology in Ireland. An architect by training, Rodd's career has spanned hospital master planning and design, spatial resource management and ageing-and-place research. Rodd's research interests are focused on understanding the interrelationship between environmental structure, ICT and people's health and wellbeing. Rodd has been very involved in the WHO's age-friendly cities movement from its inception, and is committed to improving the quality of life for older people through place-centred innovation, service improvement and social innovation. Rodd is actively involved in the European Innovation Partnership on Active & Healthy Ageing where his contribution is at the implementation interface between research, policy and practice. Rodd is a member of the Royal Institute of the Architects of Ireland.

Siobhán Cafferty is the Social Enterprise Project Manager working with the Irish Prison Service and Probation Service. Having developed the social enterprise strategy for the Department of Justice and Equality, 'A New Way Forward – Social Enterprise Strategy 2017 – 2019', Siobhán is dedicated to improving the infrastructure to support social enterprises within the criminal justice sector in Ireland. Siobhán was previously the CEO of The Bridge Project; a community based organisation working with adult males convicted of violent offences. It was as a result of her experiences in this role that Siobhán developed an interest in social enterprise initiatives as a mechanism to increase employment options for people with criminal convictions as well as assisting with the reintegration back into society following custodial sentences.

Dr Lucia Carragher is a Research Fellow in the NetwellCASALA Centre, School of Health and Science, Dundalk Institute of Technology in Ireland. Lucia has experimented in many aspects of creativity and innovation in the development and implementation of multi-stakeholder projects to support independent living for older adults. In particular, she has supported innovation in community care towards more personalised, cost-effective services to enable ageing-in-place.

Jordana Corrigan has worked in the public and private sector in the areas of spatial planning and development management. She holds a BSc in Spatial Planning and a MSc in Local Development and Innovation from Dublin Institute of Technology. Jordana has a particular interest in economic development and how improvements in technology and communications have had a transformative effect on society, and the nature and location of economic activity.

Gerard Doyle has over twenty years' experience of working in community development and social enterprise development. He has worked for an area-based partnership company, a community development network in five communities in Waterford City, and Waterford LEDC, Ireland's first not-for-profit company involving the community and corporate sector. He works as an independent research consultant, where he undertakes social research and assists communities to develop social enterprise strategies. He has lectured in community development and social enterprise development in DCU, Waterford Institute of Technology, and in a full-time basis in the Institute of Technology Blanchardstown. He is secretary of the Society for Co-operative Studies in Ireland. He holds an MSc in Local Economic Development from the University of Glasgow. He is currently doing a PhD on the role social enterprise can play in the transition to more sustainable local economies.

Deirdre Garvey is the Chief Executive Officer of The Wheel, Ireland's association of charities, community and voluntary organisations. Deirdre has represented the charity, community and voluntary sectors' shared interests on many fora over the years including the Charity Regulator's consultative panel on the 'Regulation of Fundraising (2016); the Working Group on 'Citizen Engagement in Local Government' (2013/2014); the Steering Groups for the European Years of, the Citizen (2013), and of Volunteering (2011) respectively. Previously, Deirdre was a member of the National Economic and Social Council (NESC) the Steering Group of National Social Partnership framework. She was also selected to represent the sector on the Implementation and Advisory Group of the Government's White Paper on Supporting Voluntary Activity (2000 – 2008). Deirdre was the inaugural Chairperson for the Working Group which developed, and published the Governance Code for Community, Voluntary and Charitable Organisations (2009 – 2012). She is a regular public speaker on the topics of corporate governance in nonprofits, charities regulation and best practice in charities, active-citizenship matters and all issues affecting charities and the non-profit sector. Prior to joining The Wheel, Deirdre was Director of Development (Fundraising) at The Barretstown Gang Camp in Kildare where she worked for five years. Before moving into full-time work in the community and voluntary sector in 1995, Deirdre worked in the private sector, holding several managerial posts in the hi-tech field in Germany. Having studied science for her bachelor's degree in 1986, she completed a Masters in Business Administration in 2003.

Farah Mohktareizadeh is an educator and community activist with firm roots in local and global solidarity advocacy. Passionate about working with grassroots, bottom-up projects that nurture popular struggle for social change, Farah is a Community Educator at An Cosán VCC.

Deirdre Mortell is CEO of the Social Innovation Fund Ireland. Deirdre has built Social Innovation Fund Ireland from the ground up and is also CONNECT's Social Entrepreneur in Residence at Trinity College Dublin. She has over twenty years' experience of changing the world one step at a time. Deirdre has been CEO of ONE Foundation, which granted €80 million over 2004-2013 to enable Irish and Vietnamese non-profits to make a step change in impact. She has also held senior roles in fundraising and communications in Oxfam and Barnardos, and held multiple Board directorships. At ONE Foundation, Deirdre pioneered a venture philanthropy approach in Ireland. She is co-author of "Venture Philanthropy & Social Investment: A Practical Guide". Deirdre has done 7 non-profit start-ups in the last 10 years. Uniting all this is Deirdre's passion for social change, both globally and locally in Ireland, and the power both of philanthropy and the ordinary citizen to change things – often faster than we think.

Philip McDermott is a lecturer in Sociology at Ulster University. He has a specific interest in cultural diversity, especially in relation to language. Having completed a PhD in 2008 he published a book on policy for migrant languages in Northern Ireland. Since then he has conducted a number of research projects in the North-West region with various community organisations including the North-West Migrants Forum. Philip was a Charlemont scholar of the Royal Irish Academy in 2015-2016 and is currently working on community based projects on memory and identity funded by the Arts and Humanities Research Council of the UK (AHRC).

Professor Ronaldo Munck is Head of Civic Engagement at Dublin City University and a Visiting Professor of International Development at the University of Liverpool and St. Mary's University, Nova Scotia. He has authored or edited more than 30 books on various topics related to globalisation, international development and social movements as well as over 200 academic journal articles. He serves on the editorial boards of a number of international journals including Globalizations, Global Social Policy, Global Discourse, Global Labour, Labour History, Review: Journal of the Fernand Braudel Centre, the Canadian Journal of Development Studies and Latin American Perspectives.

Thomas Murray is Pedagogy Lead at An Cosán Virtual Community College where he works in the field of higher, adult, and community education. A political scientist by training, his teaching and research interests include social justice, democracy and human rights. Thomas recently published his first book, 'Contesting Economic and Social Rights in Ireland: 1848-2016' with Cambridge University Press.

Deiric Ó Broin is Director of NorDubCo, based in Dublin City University, and Senior Research Fellow in the School of Law and Government in DCU where he lectures in Irish politics. In addition he lectures in local development and innovation at the School of Transport Engineering, Environment and Planning in the Dublin Institute of Technology. He is a graduate of the Dublin Institute of Technology (BA [Hons] and LLB), the National College of Industrial Relations (Industrial Relations Management), UCC where he obtained a MBS (Social Enterprise), Keele University, where he completed a MA (Research Ethics) and UCD, where he completed a MA (Politics and Economics) and a PhD (Political Theory). He is Chairperson of the Institute of Economic Development (Ireland Branch), a member of the Executive Committee of the Regional Studies Association (Irish Branch), and Co-Convenor of the Local Government Specialist Group of the Political Studies Association of Ireland.

Michele O'Sullivan has qualifications in financial services from the Institute of Banker's in Ireland, a bachelor's degree in business studies (DCU), and a master's degree in strategic management (DIT), Michele's most recent degree was a PhD (DIT) completed in 2016. Michele's background includes almost 20 years practical experience in financial services including marketing and strategic development roles in personal banking and home mortgages; third level lecturing experience in operations and supply chain management, human resources, childcare, business innovation and marketing; and experience, initially as a volunteer and later as general manager, in developing and establishing a social enterprise in school age childcare.

Lilian Seenoi-Barr is originally from Kenya and arrived in Derry in 2010. She then established North West Migrants Forum in 2012 and is currently the Director of Programmes. Lilian has a keen interest in the concept of intercultural dialogue and attempts to embed this in all aspects of her work. Lilian recently graduated from Ulster University with a first class BSc Hons in Community Youth Work.

FOREWORD

I am delighted to introduce this volume on social innovation in Ireland. DCU is a research intensive globally-engaged university. We take pride in our commitment to enterprise, innovation and transformation.

For me social innovation is about the translation of knowledge into societal and economic benefits. Social innovation might be seen as a novel solution to a social problem that is more effective, efficient and sustainable than current solutions. It may include new strategies, concepts and structures that better meet the needs of society.

We have a particular interest in North-South collaboration at DCU having close links with our northern counterparts. Higher education can not only do more to foster educational cross-border links but could also use its resources and partnerships to foster wider collaboration more proactively.

With the impact of Brexit still unclear, but with the likely impact being negative, we need to do all we can to promote North-South social innovation.

This volume brings together academics and practitioners across various sectors such as education, health and justice to promote just such new thinking.

I wish to commend this volume to you and urge you to engage with the North-South Social Innovation Network which is driving this work forward.

Prof Brian MacCraith
President
Dublin City University

CHAPTER 1
INTRODUCTION

Deiric Ó Broin and Ronaldo Munck

Background
This book has its birth in a series of discussions that took place
between academics with an interest in the changes taking place
in the interface between state's public service delivery systems,
civil society and service users, and those working to develop
new models of service delivery. The discussions, while initially
informal, developed into a more coherent set of thematic
dialogues, and in turn led to an agreement to establish a
network of academics, public servants, and practitioners across
the island of Ireland to provide a structure to shape the various
dialogues. The network, now called the North-South Social
Innovation Network, was launched on the 2nd November 2016
at the Dundalk Institute of Technology at a conference entitled
'Social Innovation: Lagan to Liffey'. In addition to serving as a
platform to launch the network and providing a mechanism to
facilitate networking and collaboration between those involved
in social innovation activities, the conference examined the
critical areas of funding, sustainability and the governance of
social innovation. The debates that took place on the day
persuaded the organisers that there was scope to continue the
debates and that an edited volume, based on the contributions
on the day but taking account of the dialogue between distinct
perspectives, could be a significant contribution to the ongoing
discussions about social innovation.

In this context the editors agreed to bring together
contributions from the conference and some critical
perspectives. A feature of this book, and those that preceded it is
our desire to combine academic insight with the knowledge and
experience of those involved in public policy formulation at a
variety of levels, and from different practitioner perspectives. As
Hambleton notes this can be a "hazardous enterprise as scholars
and practitioners tend to inhabit separate worlds" (2014: xiii). As
a result they can often, while speaking the same language, talk
past each other to the disadvantage of both parties. We hope

that this book helps consolidate and further the dialogue we have worked to nurture.

This introductory chapter details the broad civic and political context and focus of the book, broadly reviews the chapter themes, provides some background on the origins of the book and finally, suggests the possible contribution the book can make.

Setting the Civic and Political Context.

Some will argue that every generation believes it is facing near insurmountable challenges and living through tumultuous changes. Societies have always faced challenges. What is so different about now? The editors take the view that there are two distinct reasons why the current dynamic of change presents unprecedented challenges for those concerned with shaping public policy and delivering public services.

The first relates to the changing nature of the state in a globalising environment, or maybe more accurately the state's perception of its ability to deliver critical public services in such an environment. Since the 1970s we have witnessed an unprecedented philosophical and intellectual assault on the rationale underpinning the state's framing and delivery of public services. It may be a cliché at this stage but the post-1945 welfare state has been undermined in a manner that can be difficult to respond to. While Ireland's welfare state is quite distinctive it has not been immune to the critical discourse that has shaped politics and political oversight and management of key public services.

The second reason relates to the changes in expectation of citizens. As education participation levels have increased, dramatically in some cases, citizens have become increasing critical of the quality of services being delivered and the framework in which they are delivered. The broad social solidarity or mutualism that is seen as underpinning the modern welfare state, while not undermined, has evolved. Increasingly key social cohorts are less that enthusiastic about the type of income transfers necessary to ensure social cohesion.

Themes

This book draws together contributions from academics and practitioners in the public policy, local government, social innovation, civil society and local development sectors who contributed to the North-South Social Innovation Network Conference Social Innovation: Lagan to Liffey on Wednesday 2nd November 2016 in the Muirhevna Building in the Dundalk Institute of Technology. The conference's keynote address was delivered by Baroness Glenys Thornton, Chief Executive of the Young Foundation, UK and Deirdre Garvey, Chief Executive Officer of The Wheel, Ireland. It also included contributions from those working in the areas of justice, health, regeneration and education. Colin Mc Cabrey from Belfast City Council and Norman Thompson from Dublin City Council presented on innovation in Belfast and Dublin City Councils.

In addition to the formal academic and public policy contributions the conference was devised to include a very significant input from practitioners. This took two distinct forms, the first was a set of Thematic Workshops:

Panel 1. Social Innovation and Regeneration

Jonathan Mc Alpin (East Belfast Enterprise) *Transforming Communities in Conflict through Enterprise Education and Support.*
Andy Hallewell (Irish Central Border Area Network) *Social Innovation in Europe 'REVIVE' Transnational Project and Design Innovation Approaches.*
John Peto (Nerve Centre, Derry) *Fab Social - Making Communities Resilient.*
Paul Braithwaite (Building Change Trust) *Building an Ecosystem of Support for Social Innovation in Northern Ireland.*

Panel 2. Social Innovation and Justice

Cecilia Whitehorn (South Belfast Social Enterprise Hub) and Gillian Robinson (PBNI) *Is there a role for social enterprise Innovation in the Justice Sector?*
Siobhán Cafferty (The Bridge Project, Dublin) *Risk and Reward: Factors that Support or Inhibit the Development of Social Enterprise in the Irish Criminal Justice System.*
Seamus Carlin (Cruinn Associates) *Reshaping Systems for Families and Social Justice.*

Roger Warnock (Young Foundation, NI) *Using Social Innovation to Change People's Lives.*

Panel 3. Social Innovation and Health
Lucia Carragher and Rodd Bond (DKIT) *Leadership for Change.*
Tony Doherty (Health, Living Centres Alliance, NI) *Transforming Your Care and Making Life Better.*
Lauri McCusker (Fermanagh Trust) *Community Energy: Unleashing the Potential for Communities to Power Change.*

Panel 4. Social Innovation and Education
Emma McKenna (Queen's University Belfast), Catherine Bates (Dublin Institute of Technology) and Catherine O'Mahony (University College Cork) *The Science Shop Model for Social Innovation in Research, Teaching and Learning.*
Kevin McLoughlin (Recreate Ireland) *Creative Reuse - Making Innovation Accessible and Affordable.*
Amanda Slevin (An Cosán Virtual Community College) *A Pedagogy for Transformation: Blended Education and Social Innovation.*

The second practitioner input came from a structured plenary session facilitated by Roger Warnock (Programme Leader, Northern Ireland, Young Foundation) and Fiona Descoteaux (CEO, Innovate Dublin). The conference was also recorded and made publicly available which in turn allowed contributors to revisit points made by each other and incorporate them into the chapters in this edited volume.

A number of sometimes distinct, sometimes overlapping, and sometimes conflicting themes emerged from the conference and the subsequent discussions. The first theme relates to the importance of defining social innovation and how problematic, for a very wide variety of reasons, this is.

The second theme reflects Ireland's seeming lack of regard, despite some lip service, for social innovation. This is despite the very considerable success of many of the practitioners present at the conference. Taken in conjunction with the political culture in Ireland and Northern Ireland, a number of contributors highlight the potential and likely obstacles to implementing frameworks that might meaningfully facilitate models of social

4

innovation, in particular the politico-cultural and institutional reform constraints.

The final theme emerging from the conference and the related dialogue is the potential for disharmony and potentially conflict between key sectors in the broad social innovation space. While this relates to the definitional theme mentioned above, it is potentially more problematic and given the scare resources available in Belfast and Dublin to facilitate social innovation it suggests that a shared approach to advocacy by those in this space is not just appropriate but vitally important to their sustainability.

Book Outline
The book's contributions are structured around four distinct themes: as follows:
- Definitions;
- Ecosystems;
- Sectors;
- Social Innovation; Learnings and Perspectives
The book includes a number of chapters which were not part of the conference but the editors feel they make a valuable contribution to the discussion the book aims to facilitate. Doyle's provides a rich and contemporary set of practitioner insights and experience from the social enterprise sector, in particular the contributions of co-operative and mutual initiatives. Ó Broin highlights the challenges facing those designing public policy frameworks in Dublin and Belfast and details the problems arising from competing and conflicting definitions and the ideologies them. McDermott and Seenoi-Barr describe the practical challenges posed by cross-border working. Mortell and Garvey provide distinct practitioner perspectives, Mortell details the functioning of a social innovation fund the critical role of finance in establishing sustainable social innovations. Garvey provides a very useful civil society representative perspective on how key stakeholders in civil society are viewing debates about social innovation.

The sectoral contributions from Cafferty, Bond, Murray and Mohktareizadeh, and O'Sullivan provide rich insights from sectors for social innovation is making, or is charting a path to, substantial contributions to service delivery and user experience.

The final chapter by Corrigan reflects on the areas of definitions, risk aversion and behavioural change, research and measurement of social innovation.

We are also conscious that there a number of areas the contributors and the related discussions didn't cover, for example the relationship between politics and social innovation, how do politicians and political parties view social innovation and what shapes these views, or the role of existing actors, e.g. the credit union movements, and the potential for collaborative approaches to financial sustainability. Unfortunately, these are the constraints that arise in an initiative of this type, you only notice what you didn't discuss after the event.

We hope that the arguments advanced in this book will provide ideas and insights that can support the development of new thinking about how to develop appropriate policy frameworks and the supports that can facilitate the development of social innovation from Lagan to Liffey. As noted above the book aims to engage academic work in real policy decisions and to link the work of the university to the world of practice. In this context the book's aim is not to provide solutions but to help the reader revise and assess their own ideas.

SECTION I
DEFINITIONS

CHAPTER 2
SOCIAL INNOVATION: WHAT'S IN A NAME?

Ronnie Munck

Introduction

New terms arrive and old ones are recycled all the time, so why has 'social innovation' for a long time neglected, now come to the fore? Social innovation is widely seen as creating new approaches to address social needs that are in their ends and means and aiming towards transforming social relations. But how does this relate to social enterprise or social entrepreneurship for example? The first section of this chapter looks at definitions and what we might mean by social innovation now in Ireland so as to establish a common starting point for our discussions. The second section explores the constraints that lie on the path of social innovation, too often seen as an obvious good but then not examined critically. The third section turns to politics, too often neglected in the social innovation discourses presented in a studiously apolitical language, which obscures the contradictions in its usage. Finally the chapter addresses engagement, that is, to the participation of citizens in the social innovation processes, without which they might just become another management tool and not deliver on its transformationalist promise.

Definitions

A recent transnational European project on social innovation deemed it a "quasi-concept" (Tepsie 2014:10) which, at first glance, might come across as a somewhat dismissive description. The concept is quite unclear, and its adoption by researchers, policy makers and practitioners has been under various guises, some quite woolly indeed. It is a fluid concept and very much a hybrid, taking methods, philosophy and politics from various, possibly incompatible, sources. This flexibility may have a positive side insofar as it is infinitely adaptable to different contexts but it clearly lacks conceptual, let alone scientific, precision. This is not meant to be a dismissal of 'social innovation' as mere buzzword, devoid of any real meaning and totally vacuous. It does mean we need to deconstruct and then reconstruct its meaning to be clear on what we mean it to say. This is no different from what we have had to do in the past in relation to 'social capital' for example, whose meaning stretched from the warm and fuzzy to the hard-edged instrumental use of the concept by the World Bank (see Fine 2001). To seek clarity in a concept is a prerequisite to produce socially robust knowledge.

One of the reasons why 'social innovation' seems elusive as a concept is its apparent overlap with the other notion or practice of 'social entrepreneurship'. It seems clear that social entrepreneurship and social enterprise are subsets of the broader social innovation concept and the latter cannot be reduced to the first. We cannot simply assume that social enterprise will lead to social innovation, as is often assumed. There is a contradictory institutional logic between market oriented initiatives and socially oriented ones, for all the hype of 'social impact' amongst entrepreneurs. Public sector innovators are also often overlooked in this debate around social entrepreneurship/innovation. Nor can social innovation be subsumed under the new wave of enthusiasm for 'innovation'. An innovation with a social impact – Facebook for example - does not necessarily lead to social innovation in the sense we have defined it. Nor, for that matter, is a market-facing social innovation – Fair Trade for example – have the same significance as social innovations where markets do not exist, be it in the cultural domain or in regards to social services.

I think it is important to be wary of conceptual fuzziness or slippage as a term seemingly takes on as many meanings as the number of people articulating it. Social innovation is about creating social value, engaging citizens, having a social impact, social engagement and social inclusion. Social inclusion is a disruptive concept because it cuts across academic boundaries and policy/practice divides as well. It creates tensions and can generate new thinking if it is transgressive of conventional thinking, policies and practices. Social innovation is inherently inter-disciplinary and inter - departmental. The global social challenges – hunger, inequality, poverty, decent work, social welfare - are all 'wicked problems', that is to say not amendable to simple or self-contained solutions. Being aware of these issues we may prevent social innovation going the way of previous concepts to become so bland they are almost meaningless.

It might help clarify our own thoughts if we examined what social innovation is 'not'. As Tepsie points out "much of the existing literature is influenced by a business/technology view of social innovation" (Tepsie 2014:7). We have already mentioned the case of Facebook but we can also bring in all the various 'disruptive' business innovations of recent years as a case in point. Likewise, for example, health technologies may be innovative within their own framework but there is little sign of social innovation on the way most health systems operate or, for that matter, in constraining the market logic of the giant pharmaceutical companies. Social enterprise may refer to social value but if its logic is market logic then there is a limit to what it can achieve in terms of social innovation read as encouraging social transformation. Drawing these distinctions is not about creating a 'pure' social innovation but, rather, it is aimed at helping us to be clear on what the various constraints on social innovation are and the parameters for progressive social transformation.

Now, we can probably better try to articulate what social innovation 'is' in a way that is not dogmatic or prescriptive on the one hand or hopelessly vague on the other hand. Geoff Mulgan starts his deconstruction/reconstruction of social innovation as a concept by noting that "it is all around us", "in self-help health groups, self-build housing, microcredit and consumer cooperatives, fair trade movements and Wikipedia just for starters" (Mulgan 2007:7). A social innovation – as against technological innovation – leads to compelling new social relationships. Mulgan's definition of social innovation is disarmingly simple: "new ideas that work", (Mulgan 2007:8). He ends up with 10 'world-changing social innovations' some of which I think clearly are: the Open University (UK), the Grameen Bank (Bangladesh), Participatory Budgeting (Brazil), Linus software (Finland) and Fairtrade (UK-US). Others he lists I see as better classified as NGO's because that is what they are, namely Greenpeace, Amnesty International and Oxfam with the UK's Women's Institute hard to classify as either social innovation or NGO.

Constraints

If social innovation was easy we would see more of it, as clearly no one can be 'against' it. In reality there are many constraints in place impeding the free flow of social innovation. Some of these constraints are practical. Financing social innovation is an obvious and ever-present constraint. Social innovators are particularly dependent on their own income sources. Some may seek to operate with a market model and depend on sales, while others are dependent on grants and benefactors. In both cases there is a high degree of uncertainty, particularly in a period of crisis post 2008-2009 when things are cut down to 'core business' everywhere. The whole issue of 'scaling up' from small local level social innovation to a regional or national level is notoriously fraught and there are many impediments and constraints. An underlying issue is that it is often in those areas where the social issue is most pressing that the possibility of financing is less so and there is thus always the temptation to go for 'easy wins'.

The broader issue we need to consider is around the need to create a viable and sustainable eco-system for social innovation. Access to finance is one major constraint but research has also found that there are often clear skills deficits, poorly developed networks and a lack of proper enabling cultures preventing sustainable progress. Above all, it is seen that these are not isolated factors that can be addressed one by one but, rather, a complex set of interlocking impediments to sustainable social practices. Procurement and commissioning structures are also far from enabling good social innovation, as could be said for the whole regulatory structure under which social innovation operates. Finally, from a metrics point of view it would be true to say that there is a problem in terms of evaluating and measuring success in social innovation work. While there is no shortage of demand- social need- the provision of a robust social innovation model suffers from problems of finance, regulation and governance which are sometimes overwhelming and snuff out interesting and well-grounded initiatives.

To understand why these constraints are seemingly so intractable we need to dig deeper, I would argue, to examine the structural constraints in place. The economic historian Karl Polanyi (2001) at the end of the Second World War wrote of how capitalism advanced in a series of 'double movements' whereby the market expanded to take all social processes under its logic, but a counter-movement by society eventually fought back to re-embed economic relations within social ones. Put at its simplest, there is market logic of 'commodification'- everything can be bought and sold - and there is a social counter-logic which protects society (and nature) from the ravages caused by an un-regulated market. In terms of more recent economic history we can say that from around 1980 to say 2000, the first movement of market dominance was the period of so called neoliberalism. Since 2000, and particularly since the crisis of 2008-2009 we have seen the emergence of social counter-movements whereby society seeks to regain control of economic processes and trade, housing and health, job creation, environmental protection and so on.

We could argue, following Polanyi's 'double movement' thesis that the recent flourishing of social innovation initiatives and the social economy more broadly, is inscribed in this structural logic. These are forms of economic, political, and social solidarity that have contested the dominant market paradigm. Thus the Grameen Bank in Bangladesh began a bold experiment in rural micro-credit that was eventually 'mainstreamed' by the World Bank and others. Another hugely influential reaction to market liberalism and political authoritarianism is the participatory budget first trialled in Porto Alegre in 2005 and since extended to many parts of Brazil and internationally. At first society reacts in a protective manner, for example in relation to environmental degradation by mining companies, but then it moves towards creating protective and redistributive political structures. Reciprocal solidarity – organized through face-to-face social networks – is the key expression of this vast counter-movement that 'social innovation' is arguably part of.

We need to accept that there are inherent structural constraints impeding the small progress of social innovation and not first technical problems that could be swept aside. One of the paradoxes is that social innovation is often seen as necessary during periods of economic and political crisis, precisely when the backing needed might be least forthcoming. As Geoff Mulgan writes "A contented and stable world might have little need for innovation. Innovation becomes an imperative when problems are getting worse, when systems are not working or where institutions reflect past rather than present problems" (Mulgan 2007:9). If this is, indeed, the case we might need to grasp a crisis as an opportunity. As many financial strategists said at the time of the 2008-2009 global financial crisis: 'never let a good crisis pass you by'. The globalised, information-based and financialised world we live in is complex and open to alternatives, it is up to us to find these options and pursue them.

Politics
Many of the promoters of social innovation operate in a studiously a-political universe. It is as though, if we keep politics out, we will garner a wider coalition of forces behind the drive for social innovation. This is understandable but we simply cannot ignore the politics of social innovation and the political context in which it operates in theory and practice. So, for example, John Pearce writes about the social economy that "in the heyday was all about empowerment, about community self-help", but now "the language of the business school has usurped the language of activism and political engagement" (Pearce 2009:30). It is not a question, I would argue, about bemoaning the passing of the 'good old days" but it is necessary to be aware of the discursive politics at play in all the current debates and pitches for social innovation. Only on that basis will one be able to construct a viable and sustainable social innovation movement in Ireland.

If most political parties in most countries support social innovation do they all mean the same thing by this term? In reality there is a dearth of definitions of what is meant by social innovation/social economy both by those who promote the terms and by those who adopt them. There is a persuasive argument that governments will seek to co-opt the social economy as a 'partner' in service delivery, only paying lip service to its stated aims and objectives to construct a better society. There is a clear precedent here in the evolution of the international development NGO's. In the 1980s most international NGO's advocated bottom-up development, working with social movements in the global south and were politically independant. In the course of the 1990s as

13

neoliberalism was consolidated - and the state was forced out of many sectors - the NGO's began to fulfil a service delivery role at the behest of the international financial institutions and lost their political independence as they pulled away from social movements for radical change.

I will examine two influential social innovation networks - Ashoka Global and the Young Foundation - to seek a better understanding of the politics of social innovation. Ashoka Global (www.ashoka.org) is an international non-profit organisation which identifies and brings together leading social entrepreneurs to introduce innovative system solutions for the most pressing social problems. The network model adopted is ideally suited to sharing of information, facilitating mutual learning testing new ideas, developing models of best practice, etc. This international social innovation network undoubtedly provides a platform for collaboration and its reach can ensure greater social impact. And yet we need to ask questions from a social transformation perspective. What are the implications of any US-led international civil society initiative? What is the difference between an individual based network and a social movement for transformation? What is the difference between an enlightened top down social innovation initiative and a bottom-up one?

The Young Foundation (www.youngfoundation.org) which is UK based but with an international reach, is very much a pioneer of social innovation with projects such as the Open University in its back catalogue. It has developed a methodology for urban and regional "movement based social innovation" (Young 2016) which is methodologically innovative. It is based on a coherent theory of social change which it (correctly) believes "will be non-linear, iterative and inherently messy" (Young 2016:9). Faced with a range of social, economic and environmental challenges we cannot expect "business as usual" to deliver different results. "There is a pressing need for new responses and solutions" (Young 2016:17). One cannot but agree. But we are left with a programme for social change with no explicit political agent to deliver it. If we avoid naming the politics of the day we might maintain our neutrality (for what it's worth) but we are left with a missing ingredient: what is this social movement that will drive social innovation? What political parties, existing or in formation, will support it?

We are maybe, a bit clearer now on the complexity and contradictions – in a conceptual and political sense – of social innovation and the associated terms of the social or solidarity economy. The notion of the social economy has become mainstreamed since the crisis and we need to understand why. Governments around the world are taking what was a fringe interest in the 1970s and placing it at the core of new legislation and policies. This is partly about 'doing more with less' using society to fill the gaps left by the austerity measures taken in the wake of the crisis. But, as Ash Amin argues "This shift in mainstream thinking is not entirely of a utilitarian nature. It also stems from a desire to make capitalism more 'caring' , through markets and modes of delivery that are socially responsible, needs-based and stakeholder oriented" (Amin 2009:5). We might, with some justification, question whether capitalism can ever be reconstructed as a 'caring' socially oriented system or whether the language of 'stakeholder' is actually meaningful, but we do here get to the core of social innovation as political concept.

Next steps

In terms of building a vibrant North-South Social Innovation Network in Ireland the current conjuncture is a propitious one I would argue. Whatever happens around Brexit and the border the need for cross border co-operation will become stronger than ever. A vibrant social innovation movement, especially around the Dublin-Belfast axis, could have considerable knock-on effects across the island. The involvement of the universities, local and city authorities, community organisations and campaigning groups in a focused manner is both possible and desirable. Creating a model of best practice which utilises this energy is very achievable. This will be based on a co-operative networked way of organising as accords with the principles of social innovation; whereby the means is as important as the ends. Social innovation should not be about filling the gaps left by austerity measures and the dismantling of the welfare state but about offering alternatives to failed free market policies.

15

Engagement

Many of the proponents of social innovation refer to the need for, and advantages of, citizen engagement in its activities. As Tepsie puts it "Citizen Engagement is widely recognized as a key component to many social innovations, especially within the public sector. Citizens have growing appetite to take part in decision making processes, shape services and innovate for themselves. In response governments around the world have started to advocate higher levels of citizen engagement and experiment with various forms of engagement" (Tepsie 2013:16). There is a wide range of modalities for citizen engagement in social innovation ranging from citizen petitions, citizen juries and citizen ideas banks to competitions, crowd sourcing and crowd funding. Research is always supposed to be 'user led' although that often means industry and not citizen consultation. Groups of citizens may also be involved in piloting social innovation schemes and there is always an emphasis on user feedback once a project is completed. But is this citizen engagement and proper participation?

There is a long history of citizen engagement in international development projects that may be illuminating in this regard. For a long time participation and even empowerment – was the mantra of all NGOs and academic researchers. Their service provision would be different from that of the state precisely because they would involve the participants in some way. By the 1990s the participation one logic had even been taken up by the World Bank along with empowerment and gender equity. However, before long some more sceptical voices were writing about 'the tyranny of participation' (Cooke and Kothari 2001). There was a widespread feeling that participation was mere window-dressing and that it was not at all clear that these activities actually benefited those it was supposed to benefit. In the development of a social economy and social innovation we have good reason to be wary of top-down participation rhetoric and need to examine more critically the nature of the relationships between the citizen, the state and the various parts of civil society engaged in this activity.

While cognisant of the limitations and contradictions of citizen engagement we should also be aware of the potential benefits to society and the individual. Faced with multiple forms of social exclusion – social, cultural, economic, political – disadvantaged groups (and society) can only benefit from any measures promoting social inclusion. As austerity policies and the dismantling of many social services atomize society then any measures promoting social cohesion – for example citizen participation - need to be viewed positively. While we need to be sceptical of the conceptual inflation which occurred with the concept of 'social capital' we might accept Putnam's original argument that social capital is the glue that keeps communities together and has a wide range of positive benefits for the individual and society alike. Finally in terms of the broader question of democracy and development, research shows there are positive relationships between citizen engagement and both of these desirable outcomes for society.

The benefits of engagement to the individual are manifold. The transformative benefits of participation in any social activity are well known, from the development of skills and capabilities to the development of connections and building of social networks. Collective social action through association and activities can, indeed, lead to empowerment in a very tangible way. Many of the benefits for the individual are instrumental- networks which can help in accessing jobs or services – but they can also have a wider politicising impact. What research and experience also shows is that there is a huge difference between fairly limited and passive participation through surveys, petitions or making donations; and the wider societal benefits of bringing people together to develop and pursue collective aspiration. We still need more research on the links between participation or engagement and the outcome of particular social innovation initiatives but the general trend of the evidence is positive.

Ultimately no degree of citizen engagement will lead, in and of itself, to successful resolution of society's problems. We can say citizen engagement is beneficial to society and to the individual citizen but we cannot say that it will lead to successful social innovation; in short it is not a panacea. What we can say, based on observations internationally, is that where citizens do actively engage in the political process the prospects for democracy are better. If social innovation becomes part of a broader movement for social transformation it might well take on a stronger dynamic. If citizen engagement is simply a state policy and divorced from the wider political arena, then it will be no more than an add-on. Only when citizens engage fully in the wider process of social transformation and the democratisation of all spheres of life will they have the capacity to themselves promote and sustain social innovation in all its varied forms.

CHAPTER 3
CO-OPERATIVES AS SOCIAL INNOVATION – HOW OLDER MODELS OF SOCIAL ENTERPRISE ARE MORE RELEVANT THAN EVER

Gerard Doyle

Introduction

Ireland faces a number of socio-economic issues, including, an over-reliance on fossil fuels, inequality, unsustainable approaches to urban regeneration and unbalanced regional development. This chapter will demonstrate how social enterprise can lead to the implementation of socially innovative responses to addressing these issues. Social enterprise is a contentious concept and consequently there is a plethora of definitions cited. A broad definition of what constitutes a social enterprise will be employed which encompasses co-operatives, associations, mutuals and foundations. A social enterprise is an organisation established to achieve specific social objectives and which, in the process of achieving these objectives, is beneficial to the people, the environment and the local economy (Pearce 2009). Pearce (1993) cites a number of fundamental characteristics that social enterprises share which include: being democratic (one member one vote); being autonomous of the state and of external investors; being participatory in that its members control the governance and operation of the social enterprise; and they generate traded income from the sale of products/services. However, there is a growing cohort of social enterprises that do not place much emphasis on establishing participative decision-making structures. This can lead to the beneficiaries of this cohort of social enterprises not having any meaningful input in the social enterprises' strategy.

This chapter will first examine how social enterprises have developed socially-innovative responses to a range of issues: an over-reliance on fossil fuels; income inequality and unbalanced regional development. Case studies from a number of countries will be examined to highlight how social enterprises have made a significant contribution to addressing these issues which are affecting societies across the globe.

The chapter will conclude by detailing how the state and civil society can support social enterprise to perform a more central role in addressing the issues facing Irish society, rather than merely filling the residual role that it currently plays in facilitating the State's labour market objectives (Doyle and Lawlor 2012).

Social innovation can be defined as innovative activities and services that are motivated by the goal of meeting a social need and that are predominately developed and diffused through organisations whose primary purposes are social (Mulgan 2006). Although social innovation shares certain characteristics of the dominant concept of 'innovation' in the sense of new production processes or new products, its differences lie in the motivation for, and who benefits from the innovation (Mulgan 2006).

Social Enterprise and Renewable Energy

Pearce (1993) states that a core mission of many social enterprises is meeting the needs of their communities while not having an adverse impact on their community's environment. Hence, Amin *et al.* (2002) assert that social enterprises are ideally placed to engage in initiatives that promote environmental citizenship. Globally, renewable energy co-operatives (a form of social enterprise) are being formed. The rationale for co-operative renewable energy is that co-operatives:

- Can play an important role in increasing public acceptance of renewable energy, particularly wind energy (Walker *et al.* 2007) because the benefits to communities are visible;
- Can play a part in educating the public about renewable energy (Walker *et al.* 2007);
- Are an effective mechanism for generating employment and for rural regeneration (Barry and Chapman 2009);
- Reduce leakages from a local economy, generating a greater multiplier effect (New Economics Foundation 2002);
- Increase awareness of energy consumption (Bauwens 2013).

In 2008, Ireland imported 89% of its total energy consumption (SEAI 2010). This reliance on imported fossil fuels will have to be significantly reduced as Ireland is committed, by 2020, to generating 16% of all of its energy from renewable sources. Although energy generated from renewable sources currently comprises only a small percentage of total energy consumption, Ireland has abundant natural resources suitable for renewable energy (Feasta 2007). Indeed, communities have ample opportunities to exploit renewable energy resources in the form of biomass, wind and solar (Connolly and Vad Mathiesen 2014).

Renewable Energy Co-Operatives

Denmark

A number of EU countries have experienced a significant increase in renewable energy co-operatives. In Denmark, a high proportion of wind power capacity is generated by guilds (which are similar structures to co-operatives with the exception that member liability is unlimited). In 2002, 5,600 wind turbines which equated to 23% of Denmark's wind capacity were owned by guilds (Bolinger 2001). A key factor in the growth of mutually owned renewable energy was the formation of the Danish Association of Wind Power Guilds (DV), a non- profit association of wind farm guilds. This structure is responsible for representing the interest of members with respect to local authorities, utilities and wind-turbine manufacturers. At the beginning of this century, guilds were being offered substantial sums of money to sell their windmills and many accepted these offers. Investors then traded the existing windmills for the right to erect larger ones. As a result, there were 50,000 people who co-owned windmills in 2009, down from 150,000 at the start of the century (Maegaard 2009). To address this shift to larger wind-farms in Denmark, co-operators there have forged relationships with non-governmental agencies, and the trade union movement to secure the necessary capital to build large-scale wind farms formed as co-operatives. For example, the Middelgrunden wind co-operative (which is structured as a partnership between its' members) is an offshore windfarm comprising of twenty[1] wind turbines generating 40 MW of power. There are 10,000 investors in the co-operative living throughout Denmark, approximately, 100 of the investors are

---

[1] A utility company owns ten wind turbines (www.middelgrunden.dk).

21

from outside of Denmark (Larsen *et al.* 2006). The Copenhagen chapters of The Danish Union of Teachers and The General Workers Union bought shares to cover the electricity consumption in their own buildings (www.middelgrunden.dk). The design of the Middelgrundren wind turbine employed facilitates low cost maintenance. Critical factors in the implementation phase for Middelgrundren were the high levels of time invested in awareness-raising with non-governmental organisations, the public consultations with residents of Copenhagen and the unique partnership arrangement with a utility company, whereby the development costs were shared between both parties. The co-operative produces sufficient power to meet the electricity requirements of 40,000 households (Larsen 2006). A number of commentators have stated that there has been less public resistance to co-operatively owned off-shore wind energy project in Denmark compared to privately-owned projects[2].

The following case study, also from Denmark, highlights how co-operatives can pilot new renewable energy technology. A co-operative was established to generate heat and electricity from wood chips for 20,000 households in the town of Hillerød, 30 km north of Copenhagen, which has a population of 45,000 people. The technology entails a bio-gasification process that uses heat and air to extract wood gas (the energy source), at very high temperatures (1,200 degrees Celsius). The co-operative was connected to the national grid in Denmark (which is State-owned) within two days of application, at no cost (Lalor 2014).

This project was initiated in 2008 with the support of a government grant from the Danish Energy Agency through the Energy Technology Development and Demonstration Programme (EUDP5) for start-up funding. Its first purpose was to raise awareness about the potential of bio-gasification. At the end of the initial awareness-raising project, the Danish Energy Agency agreed to further support the project in 2010. The co-operative devised a prospectus for potential members – this included candid details about the potential benefits and failures.

---

[2] These comments were made at an international conference in Dublin in 2014 on renewable energy co-operatives organised by the Society for Co-operative Studies in Ireland.

As this was a demonstration project it was relatively risky and success was not guaranteed. The emphasis in the prospectus was on the benefits which would result if it succeeded (including the creation of jobs). The grant secured from the EUDP in August 2010 included the condition that all shares (1,050) had to be sold to local people (€1,000 per share) before December 2010 (Lalor 2014). As a result, an extensive marketing campaign was undertaken in September 2010 in order to achieve this target. The marketing process involved explanations of the bio-gasification process and was accompanied by extensive media coverage and advertising (radio broadcasting and local newspapers). Greenpeace supported the project. The marketing process was started in August 2010 and completed by December 2010. By this stage all the shares were sold, and by the following April (2011), the capital of €3 million was in place. The project has been operational since May 2014 on a test phase basis. It will become fully operational in the Autumn of 2017. Important considerations include having the support of alliances (including Greenpeace as well as other environmental groups). It was also important to continuously communicate and outline its projects to those who were investing in the project.

The Middelgrunden co-operative wind-farm and the Hillerød bio-gasification co-operative demonstrate that renewable energy co-operatives need not be restricted to small-scale projects, and that they can deploy new technology. A key factor in their success was the galvanising of local community support: central to this was the initial provision of candid information on all aspects of the projects' design to allay community members' concerns.

Germany

An innovative co-operative in an urban setting is located on the roof of the Volkswagen plant in Emsden in Germany. The council have leased the roof (for twenty-five years) off the company for an annual peppercorn rent of €1 and have installed solar panels. The power produced is sold to the national grid. Over 200 of the employees have invested an average of €1,000 each in the renewable energy co-operative and in return it allocates them an annual dividend (Worker Institute 2015).

REScoop

Throughout Europe, community renewable energy co-operatives are being established with the aim of democratising renewable energy production. Many of them have become affiliated to the REScoop network. Although the member co-operatives all subscribe to the International Co-operative Alliance principles of co-operatives, their organisational structures have changed in response to the socio-political environment in which they are located (Mendoc *et al.* 2009). For example some co-operatives, referred to as 'multi-stakeholder co-operatives', now have representatives from a range of interest groups as members. While REScoop has demonstrated the significant increase in community renewable energy co-operatives throughout the EU, Huybrechts and Mertens (2011) have identified a range of barriers to the development of renewable energy co-operatives including access to capital, a lack of awareness of the benefits of the co-operative model, consumer inertia and a dearth of acknowledgement of the role that co-operatives can perform in reducing the state's reliance on fossil fuels.

Connolly and Vad Mathiesen (2014) estimate that between 30% and 40% of the total heating requirement of Ireland's buildings could be provided by district heating systems[3]. Compared to other EU countries such as Denmark, the proportion of Ireland's buildings heated by district heating systems is extremely low. Therefore, Ireland could learn much from how Denmark implemented and operates its district heating networks. Co-operatives play a central role in the operation of district heating systems outside of Denmark's major cities (Chittum and Ostergaard 2014). As a result of the Heat Supply Act 1979[4] local authorities were obliged to formulate heating plans. This stimulated major investment in heating

---

[3] A district heating system works like a domestic central heating system only on a larger scale. Water is heated using a boiler located in a central boiling plant. The heat is distributed to the customer via an underground network of insulated pipes. The water in the network is continually circulating and therefore always available to the householder.

[4] The Heat Supply Act, 1979, stipulated that there would be municipal heat supply planning in each municipality, a new natural gas infrastructure, a substantial increase in district heating and that district heating would shift from fossil fuel boilers to combined heat and power plants and renewable energy.

networks, and local authorities were mandated to make households connect to new district heating systems[5]. However, to counterbalance being compelled to switch to district heating systems, consumer co-operatives were formed to manage them, thus ensuring consumer control (Chittum and Ostergaard 2014). As they are not-for-profit operations, heating costs were kept to a minimum: heating costs were calculated to cover costs only, prices are set annually, and any surplus is re-invested in improving the district heating system or in reducing prices. Furthermore, due to their democratic structures, members of the district heating system have an input into the running of the operation.

Ireland
An example of a renewable social enterprise district heating system is Camphill Ballytobin, part of the Camphill Communities of Ireland, which works with people with intellectual disabilities. Camphill Ballytobin provides accommodation to 85 people and includes a range of community facilities. Since 1999, the community has used biogas (produced from an anaerobic digestion plant) to supply heat to houses and the community facilities. The anaerobic digestion plant collects agricultural waste and delivers nutrient rich compost back to the farmers (Comhar and TCD 2011). Cloughjordan eco-village have installed a district heating system based on solar heat. However, policy makers could create a more supportive policy environment for communities to implement district heating systems. The above examples are the only two community-owned renewable energy district heating systems in Ireland. They are both small scale compared to their counterparts in Denmark, Finland and Germany that heat large sections of towns.

In particular, Chittum, and Ostergaard (2014) recommend the following key learning points for other countries in relation to the development and implementation of district heating systems:

---

[5] The rationale for establishing district heating systems was to make Denmark less reliant on fossil fuels.

- Local authorities should have a central co-ordinating role in the establishment and operation of district heating systems;
- Cost effectiveness tests should be broadened to take into account the benefits that accrue to citizens, society and localities from district heating companies which are consumer co-operatives;
- Credit unions could provide low cost loans underwritten by the state.

In Ireland, there are over 30 community renewable energy projects either operational or at planning stage. Many of the community renewable energy projects are incorporated as Industrial Provident Societies (Comhar and TCD 2011). For example, Drumlin Co-operative Wind Energy (referred to as Drumlin in this chapter) has erected six wind turbines located in counties Antrim, Armagh and Tyrone through raising finance from a combination of offering shares to the public and by securing social finance. Members receive an annual dividend. Rather than solely benefiting its members, as is the norm for conventional co-operatives, Drumlin provides funding to community projects in the locality of each turbine. Energy4all, a co-operative based in Cumbria which specialises in supporting communities to establish community renewable energy co-operatives, played a pivotal role in organising the share prospectus. Unfortunately, the UK government financial schemes which make community energy projects financially sustainable have been terminated, therefore, it is currently far more difficult to implement renewable energy co-operatives in the north of Ireland.

Social Enterprise and Inequality
Wilkinson and Pickett (2009) provide ample evidence of the corrosive influence of inequality on societies. For example they demonstrate that the countries with the highest level of income inequality experience higher incidences of: mental health issues including anxiety and depression within their respective populations; illegal drug consumption; children and adults experiencing obesity; teenage births and lower literacy attainment. In addition, more unequal countries experience

26

higher levels of violence and homicide (Wilkinson and Pickett 2009).

Erdal (2011) debunks the myths prevalent among mainstream economists concerning co-operatives and employee-owned companies realising inferior economic performance to the dominant capitalist enterprise entity because senior management is not sufficiently rewarded. Furthermore, Craig and Pencavel (1995) provide evidence that worker co-operative are as productive as capitalist firms.

Co-operatives are an important mechanism for achieving more egalitarian societies (Ranis 2016; Wilkinson and Pickett 2009:253) assert, in the transition to more equal societies, a co-operative brings a number of socio-economic advantages when compared to a capitalist enterprise:

> First it enables a process of social emancipation as people become members of a team. Second, it puts the scale of earning differentials under democratic control: if the body of employees want big income differentials they could choose to keep them. Third, it involves a very substantial redistribution of wealth from external shareholders to employees and a simultaneous redistribution of the income for that wealth. Fourth, it improves productivity and has a competitive advantage. Fifth, it increases the likelihood that people will regain the experience of being part of a community. And sixth, it is likely to improve social ability in wider society.

There is a wealth of research supporting the above assertions as illustrated by the following example. Erdal (2000) researched the impact of employment in co-operatives on communities in three Northern Italian towns. The research findings showed that indicators of health, education, social involvement, crime and social perceptions were significantly more positive in the town where co-operatives employed a larger percentage of the population.

Resilience of Co-Operatives

Many mainstream economists and policy makers criticise co-operatives for not being as financially resilient as capitalist enterprises. Regarding the survival rates of co-operatives, Birchall and Ketilson (2009:29-30) referred to the Quebec Federal Government's commissioned research in 2008 which highlighted that co-operatives have lower failure rates than capitalist enterprises. The report states that

> More than 6 out of 10 co-operatives survive more than five years, as compared to almost 4 businesses out of 10 for the private sector in Québec and in Canada in general. More than 4 out of 10 co-operatives survive more than 10 years, compared to 2 businesses out of 10 for the private sector.

Furthermore, in Germany the failure rate among co-operatives is far lower than capitalist enterprises; in 2005, 1% of capitalist businesses were declared insolvent, while the figure for co-operatives was less than 0.1% (Birchall and Ketilson 2009).

Ranis (2016) argues that the precariat, comprised of unskilled labour, and the traditional working class would benefit most from the empowerment of workers which results from the participation of worker co-operatives. The author calls for public policy to support alternative enterprise entities and for communities and social movements to coalesce in demanding for this shift in public policy. The author asserts that co-operatives share core characteristics:

- They are formed to address a shared need be it unemployment or the economic marginalisation of their communities;
- They entail participatory involvement in the management of enterprises;
- Worker owners learn to take responsibility for their actions;
- They promote economic equality as the pay differentials between senior management and ordinary workers are significantly lower than in the capitalist firm. They have the potential to weaken the two-tier wage system which

discriminates against women, immigrants and low skilled workers;

- They have the potential to strengthen working class consciousness and solidarity. Citizens would no longer see themselves as passive and atomised;
- Co-operative workers are committed to participating in wider struggles against repressive state policies.

Ranis (2016) believes that working class communities in Europe and North America can learn from the process of worker co-operative development in Argentina. The alliances between Argentinian worker co-operatives, civil society groups and influential individuals have resulted in a social movement the objective of which is to influence state institutions to introduce more supportive legislation towards co-operatives. These social movements are also required to protect the nascent worker co-operative movement against adversarial interest groups such as employers' organisations and conservative trade union bureaucrats (Ranis 2016). Over time, a mutually beneficial relationship can emerge between co-operatives and communities in which the co-operatives are based as exemplified in the Zanon worker co-operative in Buenos Aires. Moreover, the co-operatives can contribute to strengthening egalitarian values among the body politic. Ranis (2010) emphasises the importance of 'eminent domain' (the expropriation of private property for public benefit) in allowing fledgling worker co-operatives in South America and the USA with the opportunity to secure the assets required to continue the manufacture of products formerly produced by investor-owned companies. These often-profitable capitalist firms move their operations to destinations with lower labour costs (Ranis 2016). Public policy needs to enshrine eminent domain in law to prevent capitalist firms moving their operations and leaving communities economically decimated (Ranis 2006).

The Italian Experience
State legislation, as exemplified by Italy, performs a key enabling role for the growth of the co-operative sector. The Italian constitution of 1945 recognised co-operatives (Zamagni 2010). This provided the bedrock for legislation supporting the development of co-operatives from 1946 onwards. The first law

introduced which defined the rules for cooperatives (one member/one vote, a minimum of nine members, a prohibition on members who had a private business in the same field, a ban on distribution of indivisible reserves, even in the event of liquidation of co-operatives). The legislation allowed co-operatives to be eligible for the subsidies that the national or local governments would distribute (Zamagni 2010). Subsequent legislation in the 1970's recognised members' loans as performing a pivotal role in increasing capital available to co-operatives. This enabled the co-operatives in Italy to achieve a dominant position in retail distribution in Italy (Zamagni 2010).

Legislation introduced in 1977 allows the surpluses of Italian co-operatives to be placed in indivisible reserves which are exempt from corporate taxation. This piece of legislation strengthens the capacity of co-operatives to become less reliant on external debt finance. Social cooperatives, which were governed by a multi- stakeholder board enabled this category to service the needs of communities rather than members alone by legislation introduced in 1991 (Zamagni 2010). Legislation in 1992 further galvanised the co-operative sector in Italy by allowing co-operatives to have members whose sole function was to provide capital. Another important piece of legislation was the introduction of an obligation on co-operatives to devote 3% of their surpluses to a fund managed by each of the umbrella organizations, described below. The purpose of this is to strengthen the co-operative movement through the creation of new co-operatives and the restructuring of some of the existing ones (Fici 2010).

Balanced regional development: Emilia-Romagna
A criticism levelled at co-operatives is lack of scale and the capacity to generate surplus income (Restakis 2010). The case study presented will demonstrate that co-operatives can achieve significant scale and contribute to regional economic development.

Emilia-Romagna is a Northern region of Italy with a population of 4.4 million (www.istat.it/en/emilia-romagna). After the Second World War, it was among the poorest regions in Italy. Today it is has achieved the highest GDP in Italy and one of the highest in Europe. Its per capita income is 30% higher than the national average and 27.6% higher than the EU average (Lappe 2006). Co-operatives have performed a vital role in the transformation of the region's economy (Thompson 2003).

In 1945, the infrastructure and economy of Emilia-Romagna was devastated. Many of the co-operative movement's leadership were killed fighting the fascist dictatorship. The socialist tradition, either in the form of communist or social democratic administrations, has had a profound influence over the region's co-operative development (Restakis 2005). There has been a continuous socialist administration since the end of the Second World War. According to Restakis (2005:2)

> What has been most remarkable however, is the capacity of this North Italian brand of civil social democracy to transform the philosophical and operational character of the industrial firm by merging the values of civil society and community with the industrial requirements of small firm capitalism.

This unique relationship has led to an inculcation of co-operation and reciprocity between capitalist firms and co-operatives, often referred to as the Emillian model, which has led to co-operative networks being formed to export manufactured goods. This relationship was reinforced by the paucity of investment in large-scale industrial plants which led to small enterprises being established (Rinehart 2009). Income distribution is also among the most equitable in Italy, with the Emilia-Romagna region maintaining a GINI Coefficient of .242 (as compared to .370 for Italy as a whole. Cornia *et al.* 2005). The economy has attained high levels of diversification (Logue 2006). The enterprises utlilise an approach of flexible specialisation whereby small and medium sized capitalist enterprises and co-operatives share expertise in various sectors of the economy. This enables the Emilia- Romagna economy to be more adaptable and resilient to changes in the external environment (Rinehart 2009).

Co-operatives are the other core component of the Emilia-Romagna economic success (Rinehart 2009). The sectors in which co-operative firms are strongest include retail, construction, agricultural production, housing, manufacturing, and social services. In the first three of these sectors, co-operatives predominate (for example in construction, agriculture, and retail). There are about 2,700 worker co-operatives in the region, accounting for 6% of the total workforce. Worker co-operatives constitute a number of the larger manufacturing companies in the region providing a bedrock for smaller co-operatives to gain contracts, retaining employment in the region and ensuring wealth does not leak out of the Emilia-Romagna (Restakis 2007). Compared to other regions of Italy, there is a high level of consumer co-operatives. Of Italy's 43,000 cooperatives, 15,000 are located in Emilia-Romagna making it one of Europe's most concentrated co-operative sectors (Borzaga *et al.* 2015).

In Bologna for example, two out of three citizens are members of a cooperative, with most belonging to several (Thompson 2003). Co-operatives directly account for over 40% of the region's GDP (Rinehart 2009). Most public works, including large-scale engineering, construction, and heritage restoration projects, are carried out by building co-operatives owned by their employee members. Co-operatives in Emilia-Romagna are linked to the key co-operatives that trade throughout Italy:

- Coop Italia is the top retailer surpassing Carrefour in sales. It has 6 million owner/members, 55,000 employees, 1,200 stores, and €11 Billion in sales. It purchases a high proportion of its produce from producer co-operatives;
- The cooperatives have their own insurance company — Unipol, large investment funds such as Coop Fund provide loan and equity to start-up companies, and very sophisticated support organizations such as Lega Coop (P2P Foundation);
- 'Social Cooperatives' provide various services to people with mental and physical disabilities. They have secured 85% of the municipalities' social service budget for Emilia-Romagna (Thompson 2003).

The region's agricultural co-ops are Europe's leaders in organic food production and in the utilisation of environmentally-friendly pest control.

Since the start of the twentieth century co-operatives in Italy have developed along ideological lines, with one principal strand aligned to the socialist tradition and the other main strand influenced by Catholic social teaching (Zamagni 2010). The former is aligned to Legacoop Emilia-Romagna, which is part of the National League of Cooperatives and Mutuals (Lega Nazionale delle Cooperative e Mutue). Legacoop is the principal association representing co-operatives in Emilia-Romagna, with its 1,250 affiliate enterprises operating across industry, agriculture and services sectors of the economy. Its member co-operatives employ over 150,000 people and represent 2.8 million shareholders (producers, workers, consumers, inhabitants, users, retailers). It has several functions:

- Promotes co-operative values and identity in the region;
- Coordinates the activities of the different Legacoop territorial and sector associations;
- Advocates on behalf of its members co-operatives with regard to public institutions, business representative bodies and trade unions at regional level;
- Assists with the formation of new co-operatives and their development through the provision of advisory services, it supports innovation, and economic cooperation processes among cooperatives. The association is also in charge for monitoring the operations of co-operatives on behalf of the Italian Ministry of Economic Development (www.emilia-romgana.legacoop.it).

Co-operatives encounter a number of obstacles in trading in markets which are dominated by capitalist enterprises (Miller 2006). Lega Coop has formed a number of secondary co-operatives to address these challenges. Fincooper is a cooperative bank which is jointly owned by consortia, co-operative depositors and Legacoop. With regard to access to capital, Fincooper, through the provision of direct loans and financial guarantees, enables co-operatives to secure different types of finance below market rates. Instituto Cooperative per L'Innovazione (LICE) which undertakes relevant research on behalf of co-operatives in construction, manufacturing and agriculture which can enable them to diversify their product and service offerings (Rinehart 2009). Another key function that Lega

Coop performs is fostering inter-co-operative purchasing of products and services. This has significantly strengthened the co-operative sector's sustainability.

Conclusion

The experiences of Denmark and Italy demonstrate the central role that social enterprise could play in a switch from a fossil-fuel-dependent economy; the creation of a more equal society and more balanced regional economies. In order for this to become a reality new partnerships between communities and other parties, including trade unions, the credit union movement and third level institutions need to be formed.

All of the political parties should have social enterprise as a core component of their economic manifestos rather than the residual role it is currently afforded. The various arms of the Irish State will have to take a more pro-active approach with regard to social enterprise development. In particular, it will have to treat social enterprise on a par with multi-nationals.

Perhaps the greatest challenge is to address the pervasive culture of individualism and consumerism which has taken root in Irish society. This cultural change will require, a number of interventions by community organisations, trade unions and progressive political parties to demonstrate that another Ireland is possible where the benefits of our economy are not unequally apportioned on the basis of class.

CHAPTER 4
TOWARDS A EUROPEAN-STYLE SOCIAL ECONOMY OR IRISH-STYLE SOCIAL INNOVATION?
CHALLENGES FOR IRISH PUBLIC POLICY

Deiric Ó Broin

Introduction

Peter Utting recently observed that the global economic crises, growing social and economic inequality and climate change have prompted "a global debate on the meaning and trajectory of development" (2015:1). This debate has seen increasing attention focused on the 'social economy' as a distinctive approach to human-centred sustainable economic development.

There is considerable evidence that policy makers are beginning to understand what the social economy is, what it promises and how it differs from 'business as usual' (European Commission 2011; UNRISD 2012). However, we know far less about whether it can really move beyond its fringe status in many countries and regions. Under what conditions can the social economy scale-up and scale-out, i.e. expand in terms of the growth of social economy organisations and enterprises, or spread horizontally within states? This chapter aims to (a) contribute an Ireland-focused response to some of these questions, (b) identify some of the definitional and categorisation challenges facing policy makers and politicians in Ireland, (c) outline the potential for the development of the social economy and (d) highlight some of the obstacles to the development and implementation of appropriate public policy interventions.

The chapter begins with a brief outline of the analytical perspective adopted, political economy, and then examines the contested concepts of 'social economy', 'social enterprise', 'social entrepreneur' and 'social innovation'. The chapter then reviews the four concepts and locates them within two distinct approaches, the first a broad approach to economic development based on economic and social solidarity and a more democratised society, and the second an evolution of the recent marketisation of the management and delivery of many public services. The chapter then briefly examines the political context in which the debate is taking place in Ireland and how it might be progressed. This is followed by an examination of two short case studies, the first, a recent effort in privately-supported social innovation in the United States and the consequences for civil society and citizens when states make decisions about the role of social enterprises without thinking through the ramifications of the policy interventions in a coherent manner. The second case study reviews the expansion and relative decline of student-owned social enterprises in Ireland and the critical role and unforeseen consequences of public policy interventions. This is followed by an examination of the current discourse and the likely consequences for public policy in Ireland.

The Role of Political Economy as a Framework for Analysis

When the concept of political economy emerged in the 18th century, it "did so to help people understand and cope with a dramatic change in the system of want satisfaction, both in the nature of wants and in the manner of production and distribution of goods for satisfying them" (Caporasa and Devine 1992:1). The latter half of the 20th century saw a distinct lack of debate about political economy and the complex and integrated relationship between politics and economics was often left in a limbo as academic and professional economists and political scientists developed more segregated and very often insular lines of discourse and debate.

The importance of political economy lies in the broader framework it provides for a discussion about the responsibilities of the state with regard to the economy. For example what is the role of the idea of a self-regulating market and what is the relationship between public ends and private interests? Different notions of economics and politics lead to different political economies? It is the contention of this chapter that the discussion about the social economy is best situated in the realm of political economy rather than the more constrained parameters of business disciplines such as management or entrepreneurship. Restakis's observation is pointed in this regard and contends that the growth in interest in the social economy lies in "ultimately the failure of contemporary political and economic

36

policies to provide minimum acceptable levels of economic and social well being to growing numbers of people" (2006:1). Isolating a discussion about the social economy from politics is both misleading and unlikely to lead to any helpful outcome.

Key Concepts
At this stage it is important to note that many use the terms 'social economy, 'social enterprise', 'social entrepreneur' and 'social innovation' interchangeably. This can be problematic and there is a very definite vagueness inherent in much of the debate in Ireland. For many 'social innovation' is an activity carried out by 'social entrepreneurs' who have established 'social enterprises' that operate in the broader 'social economy'. This perspective has the attractive characteristics of being neat, succinct and easy to comprehend. This chapter contends that, unfortunately, it is more complex and there are a variety of very different and often mutually exclusive perspectives that require critical engagement with. It is hoped that this chapter will contribute to the broader debate about the potential and actual nature and role of social enterprise, social entrepreneurs and social innovation in Ireland and a fuller understanding of the social economy and its potential contribution to social, economic and civic wellbeing.

Social Economy
In a European context the idea of a social economy is historically linked to popular associations and co-operatives. The dynamic underpinning the establishment of these organisations was a system of values and principles interlinked as an "expression of a single impulse: the response of the most vulnerable and defenceless social groups, through self-help organisations, to the new living conditions created by the development of industrial society in the 18th and 19th centuries" (Monzón and Chaves 2012:13).

Although the social economy was relatively prominent in most of Europe during the first third of the 20th century, the post-1945 growth model mainly featured the traditional private sector and the public sector. This model was the basis of the welfare state, which addressed "recognised market failures and deployed a package of policies that proved highly effective in correcting them: income redistribution, resource allocation and anti-cyclical policies" (Monzón and Chaves 2012:15). All of these were based on the Keynesian model in which the significant social and economic actors, i.e. employers' federations and trade unions, worked together with government in corporatist or quasi-corporatist arrangements (Laville 2015).

Interestingly, during this period the social economy lost its significant role in the process of "harmonising economic growth with social welfare" (Monzón and Chaves 2012:17), with the state occupying centre stage. It was not until the crisis of the welfare state in the 1970s that some European countries saw a reawakening of interest in the typical organisations of the social economy, whether business alternatives to the models of the capitalist and public sectors, such as co-operatives and mutual societies, or non-market organisations – mostly associations and foundations. This interest sprang from the difficulties that the market economies were encountering in finding satisfactory solutions to such major problems as massive long-term unemployment, social exclusion, welfare in the rural world and in run-down urban areas, health, education, the quality of life of pensioners, sustainable growth and other issues. These are social needs that are not being sufficiently or adequately addressed by either private capitalist agents or the public sector, and for which no easy solution is to be found through self-adjusting markets or traditional macroeconomic policy. For the purposes of this chapter this provides the basis for a useful understanding of the social economy, i.e. economic activity in between market and state oriented towards meeting social needs (Amin 2009; Noya and Clarence, 2007).

Social Enterprise

The term social enterprise typically refers to for-profit organisations with a social mandate, it can also include other legal forms such as non-profit organisations, charities, co-operatives, and hybrid organisations (OECD 2013). However, the term has been defined in a wide variety of ways. For example in the United States the term is normally used to refer to "market-oriented economic activities serving a social goal" (Defourny and Nyssens 2006:4). In this context the social enterprise is viewed as an innovative response to the funding problems of non-profit organisations, which are finding it difficult to solicit private donations and philanthropic grants (Dees 1998). As noted above European countries have a rather different experience of the social economy and the term social enterprise tends to be used in a different manner[6] and focuses not just on the explicit aim of benefiting a community but on the fact that it is initiated by a group of citizens (Borzaga and Defourny 2001). The recent approach by the Irish state to define a social enterprise is interesting in this regard as it excludes the nature of the establishment as a criterion, in this regard it adopts a more American understanding, and defines a social enterprise as an organisation:

- That trades for a social/societal purpose;
- Where at least part of its income is earned from its trading activity;
- Is separate from government; and
- Where the surplus is primarily re-invested in the social objective (Forfás 2013:10).

This approach is much more in keeping with the Anglo-American perspective (Ó Broin 2014) and while not excluding organisations such as credit unions or co-operatives, key components in the European social economy, is so expansive as to suggest that the state is not particularly focused on supporting the establishment of a European-style social economy but rather more interested in facilitating the growth of a more US-influenced social impact and social mission-oriented sector[7].

Social Entrepreneur
Like the term social enterprise, social entrepreneurship has, increasingly, become a catch all term: it has "become so inclusive that it now has an immense tent into which all manner of socially beneficial activities fit" (Martin and Osberg 2007:28). For

---

[6] The term was initially employed in Italy and was closely linked with the co-operative movement. In 1991 Italy adopted a law creating a specific legal form for 'social co-operatives' which were established to respond to the needs that had not been adequately met by public services (Borzaga and Santuiri 2001).
[7] This gives rise to the question if the Irish state has decided to ignore the "quest for more economic democracy that characterizes the field of social enterprise in Europe" (Defourny and Nyssens 2010:47).

the purposes of this chapter it is helpful to contrast social entrepreneurship to traditional entrepreneurship. Stated simply, entrepreneurs innovate. Social entrepreneurship distinguishes itself from entrepreneurship only insofar as the term 'social' modifies the goals and activities undertaken thereof. Entrepreneurs in business are primarily concerned with maximizing profit, whereas social entrepreneurs are motivated – in whole or in part – by social goals[8].

As such, this chapter suggests it is helpful to use the description social entrepreneurs use for themselves as entrepreneurs who "develop new, innovative solutions to address the entrenched social and environmental challenges we face" (Social Entrepreneurs Ireland 2017). As we will see in the following sections, this depiction is not as straightforward as one might expect, there are many significant questions that arise from this approach.

Social Innovation

In its August 14th 2010 edition *The Economist* included an important article on governments' interest in what it termed 'social innovation' and the role of social entrepreneurs. Central to the article was the observation that social innovation "differs from the fashion of the past couple of decades for contracting out the delivery of public services to businesses and non-profit groups in order to cut costs, in that it aims to do more than save a few dollars or pounds – although this is part of the attraction. The idea is to transform the way public services are provided, by tapping into the ingenuity of people in the private sector, especially social entrepreneurs" (2010:51). Social entrepreneurs develop "innovative answers to a social problem" (Ibid).

It was suggested that the fresh, businesslike ideas of social entrepreneurs will bring about the productivity miracle in the "social sector", defined as the public sector plus service delivering charities, similar to the one that began in businesses in the 1990s[9].

---

[8] The Global Entrepreneurship Monitor uses a similar approach in its research (Bosma *et al*. 2016).
[9] Muhammad Yunus, founder of Grameen, and Wendy Kopp, founder of Teach for America, are portrayed as representatives of this new approach. Michael Edwards used the term "Philanthrocapitalism" to describe a similar, though not

In this context one might begin to appreciate how devising a helpful working definition of 'social innovation', is in some ways, a more difficult challenge than either social enterprise or social entrepreneurship. The academic literature employs the term as a broad inclusive term and a sub-set of both social enterprise and social entrepreneurship[10]. For example the *Center for Social Innovation* at Stanford University describes social innovation as "the process of inventing, securing support for, and implementing novel solutions to social needs and problems" (Phills *et al.* 2003:1). In this context it is not the "prerogative or privilege of any organisational form or legal structure" (Ibid). To be considered a social innovation, a process or outcome must meet two criteria:

- Novelty;
- Improvement.

Although social innovations need not "necessarily be original", they must be new to the user, context, or application (Ibid) and to be considered an innovation, a process or outcome must be either more effective or more efficient than pre-existing alternatives[11]. In a similar vein Llie and During define "social innovation as new ideas (products, services, and models) that

---

synonymous, process of applying business principles to the world of civil society and noted that this process had "fashion, wealth, power and celebrity behind it" (2009:11). He described the Bill and Melinda Gates Foundation and the Clinton Global Initiative as good examples of this approach to social progress. LaMarche contends that what separates these newer social entrepreneurs or philanthrocapitalists from the likes of Carnegie is "their emphasis on measurability, on incorporating lessons from the business world" (2009:23). Matthew Bishop and Michael Green's book *Philanthrocapitalism – How The Rich Can Save the World and Why We Should Let Them* adds another characteristic, the harnessing of the "profit motive to achieve social good" (2008:6).

[10] Work by the UK Government's Office of the Third Sector neatly encapsulates the definitional confusion, in a report entitled *How can innovation in social enterprise be understood, encouraged and enabled?* The author strives to explain how "social enterprise innovation is not the same as 'social innovation'" (Westhall 2007:2).

[11] Phills *et al.* contend that innovation is both a process and a product and that "it is essential to distinguish four distinct elements of innovation". First, the process of innovating, or generating a novel product or solution, which involves technical, social, and economic factors. Second, the product or invention itself – an outcome that we call innovation proper. Third, the diffusion or adoption of the innovation, through which it comes into broader use. Fourth, the "ultimate value created by the innovation" (2008:3).

simultaneously meet social needs (more effectively than alternatives), create new social relationships and collaborations to enhance society's capacity to act" (2012:21).

From this perspective social innovation, unlike social entrepreneurship and social enterprise, is a process and creator of solution-oriented social collaborations/networks. It is argued it "transcends sectors, levels of analysis, and methods to discover the processes that produce lasting impact" (Phills *et al.* 2008). That is, social innovation covers a wider scope in addressing and solving social problems. Social entrepreneurship focuses on the personal qualities of people who start new organisations with traits like boldness, accountability, resourcefulness, ambition, persistence, and unreasonableness (Llie and During 2012:31). By contrast, the field of social enterprise tends to focus on organisations with primarily social objectives whose surpluses are principally reinvested for those purposes in the business or in the community (Kaderabkova and Saman 2013).

This approach is not without its critics and is argued to legitimise political decisions to outsource heretofore publicly-funded welfare provision to private or quasi-social actors rather than support substantive actors in the social economy (Fougère *et al.* 2017). In addition, many innovators in the social economy, managing and leading social enterprises are addressing market failures and their consequences (Lindblom 2001) and are far less enamoured with market-based solutions than suggested.

Problematising Definitions and Politico-Economic Perspectives
In addition to the problems of agreeing shared definitions of key elements of the social economy v social enterprise v social entrepreneurship v social innovation debate (Brouard and Larivet 2010), the terms are also used within the literature to describe, in addition to reflecting, distinct politico-economic perspectives. Ridley-Duff and Bull (2016:5) clearly delineate three distinct "schools of thought" that have come to dominate the academic literature. The first, linked closely to the field of entrepreneurship, is called, rather confusingly for the purposes of this chapter, social innovation (Austin *et al.* 2006; Perrini 2006). In this school of thought, entrepreneurs are presented as "heroes" (Ridley-Duff and Bull, 2016:6) and drivers of change.

The second school of thought is linked to the first in its emphasis on understanding and developing social entrepreneurs but differs in that there is a very particular emphasis placed on their value propositions and social missions (Nicholls 2008; Martin and Osberg 2007). As Ridley-Duff and Bull note, these value propositions are translated into social purposes, and the definition of the purpose becomes the foundation for an agreement on social objects. The third school of thought emphasises the creation of social enterprises that have socialised ownership and control. This is seen as crucial to "meet the commitment to democratic principles of organisation and participation in decision-making (Defourny 2010). This 'socialisation' school of thought is strongly influenced by the concept of the European social economy and sees a clear distinction between the "reciprocal interdependence that underpins mutual aid" and the "philanthropy that underpins charity" (Ridley-Duff and Southcombe 2012). Mutuality implies a bi-directional or network relationship in which parties help, support and supervise each other. This is "qualitatively different" from the uni-directional relationship between owner-manager and employee in a private enterprise, or "chain of control (philanthropist to trustee (unpaid), trustee to manager, manager to worker, and worker to beneficiary) in a charity" (Ridley-Duff and Bull 2016:7)[12].

One might ask why the continued desire to differentiate between the dynamics underpinning, what appear to be socially worthwhile and valuable, socio-economic initiatives is important or even useful. The chapter contends there are at least two important rationales. The first relates to the formulation of public policy. It is critical that those tasked with creating a policy framework for facilitating the growth of the social economy in Ireland, particularly in light of the launch of the European Commission's Social Business Initiative (2011), clearly comprehend the distinctions between various initiatives, and

---

[12] This is not to deny that charity can be present in mutual relations. However, it usually framed in law and practice as a financial and managerial one-way relationship in which trustees give and direct while beneficiaries accept and obey. It is this "asymmetry in obligations", i.e. the lack of reciprocal interdependence, that distinguishes mutuality from charity (Ridley-Duff and Bull 2016:7).

how the distinct drivers for the establishment of these initiatives will require different levels and types of support. The second rationale relates to the politico-economic sphere. The chapter contends that it is important that both critics and advocates of the broader social economy in Ireland are cogent and coherent in their use of terminology. While support for the socialisation of ownership and control is an explicitly political stance[13], it is a political stance situated well with the European Social Democratic and Christian Democratic mainstream, but in a political culture like Ireland's there is a tendency to avoid clarity if possible so as not to limit the size of the potentially supportive coalition one may assemble. The problem with such an approach is that it can lead to the achievement of a 'lowest common denominator-type solution' rather than an 'optimal solution' (Ó Broin 2015). As a result, the chapter suggests that honesty about one's motives may, in this case at least, be the best policy.

In recommending the continued need for clarity about the distinction between a socialisation perspective that emphasises collective action and mutualist principles to develop an alternative economy (Sahakian and Dunand 2015) and a social innovation and/or social purpose perspective that focuses on the missions and innovations of individual social entrepreneurs (Dees 1998)[14], it is important to note that these 'schools of thought' are not necessarily in opposition to each other. As Figure 4.1 shows many successful organisations can have distinct (a) social innovation, (b) social mission (purpose and impact) and (c) socialisation of ownership and control, elements[15]. However, it remains important to highlight the differences between the perspectives because, first, it is always useful to understand distinct strands within the development of social enterprises, and second, an organisation's overwhelming commitment to any one of them may well lead to an inability to develop a long-term sustainable future for the organisation.

---

[13] As distinct from state or private ownership.
[14] The social innovation/purpose perspective tends to emphasise the philanthropic impulse of the social entrepreneur and the social goals of the enterprise (Scofield 2011) while the socialisation perspective tends to "emphasise organisation design and stakeholder governance to educate members for participation in the social economy" (Moreau and Martens 2013).
[15] Probably the most famous example is the Mondragon Corporation in the Basque country (see http://www.mondragon-corporation.com/en/ for details).

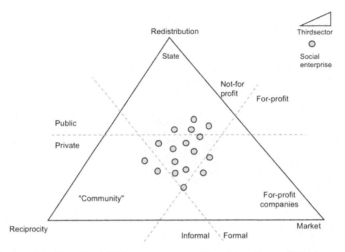

Figure 4.1: The Social Economy as a Combination of Various Actors, Logics of Action and Resources (Defourny and Nyssens 2012)

Political Context

For the purposes of this chapter it is helpful to situate the current debate in Ireland's distinctive political context[16]. On one hand there exists the components of a potentially robust and facilitative support framework for the social economy:

- Ireland has the highest per-capita credit union membership in the world;
- Historically Irish civil society has supported the establishment of human-centred economic and social institutions and activities (Ó Broin and Kirby 2009);

---

[16] The calamity facing the Irish economy in the 1980s is more widely understood at this stage and the fact that it helped to initiate a new form of public governance is accepted by the majority of political scientists. What is interesting is that Ireland did not follow the neo-liberal route chosen by many other countries in the Anglo-American sphere. The current situation is very interesting for those involved in the debate about the potential nature and role of the social economy. Despite the resilience of many of the institutions of social partnership to previous upheavals, the scale and multi-stranded nature of the recent crises has been fatal. The institutional framework of social partnership is gone and while some of the outlines of a new model of public deliberation and economic governance exist, there is little political momentum to replace social partnership.

- There is significant philanthropic support for social economy-linked organisations;
- It retains an extensive nationwide network of rural agri-business and community service co-operatives;
- The state funds a very significant social enterprise support programme, one of the largest in the European Union;
- National civil society representative organisations are actively calling for the development of a more supportive public policy framework to expand the social economy.

Despite the above the social economy is widely accepted to be underdeveloped in Ireland, representing only 3% of GDP compared to 4%-7% in other EU member states (Forfás 2013). In addition Irish public policy retains a very strong and distinct pro-private enterprise bias (Kirby 2010) and calls for support for the social economy are often perceived as attempts to undermine private enterprise and the role of the market. In addition Irish public policy efforts in this area tend to use the market-oriented discourse of 'social entrepreneurship' rather than the more society-oriented discourse of 'social economy' (Ó Broin 2012). As the situation evolves a variety of social, economic, civic, governmental and political processes and issues will impact key decisions. These include:

- The strong desire on the part of civil society to establish a robust social economy component of the national economy;
- The openly pro-market bias of many Irish government agencies;
- The economic, financial and policy constraints imposed as a result of the austerity programme;
- The highly open nature of the Irish economy, one of the most globalised in the world;
- The advocacy actions of existing social economy actors;
- The outcome of debates between proponents of social entrepreneurship and social economy;
- The establishment of appropriate national social economy support agencies;
- The implementation of the local government reform process and its social economy support function;

- The political decisions taken by the current government. This chapter uses the framework developed by Erik Olin Wright (2013) to examine the potential for the development of the social economy. His analysis provides a powerful conceptualisation of the developmental potential offered by the social economy and the instrumental effectiveness offered by reordering many economic activities to improve their impact. In relation to the social economy Wright's key argument is that the development of the social economy can constitute an interstitial transformation, i.e.

> ... new forms of social empowerment in capitalist society's niches and margins, often where they do not seem to pose any immediate threat to dominant classes and elites (2013:20).

The central theoretical idea is that building alternatives on the ground in whatever spaces are possible both serves a critical ideological function by showing that alternative ways of working and living are possible, and "potentially erodes constraints on the spaces themselves" (Wright 2013:20). Wright (2010) suggests that the social economy may also be conceived as a "real utopia" since it presents a plausible vision of a radical alternative and a project of emancipatory social change:

> The 'social economy' constitutes an alternative way of directly organizing economic activity that is distinct from capitalist market production, state organized production, and household production. Its hallmark is the production organized by collectivities directly to satisfy human needs not subject to the discipline of profit- maximization or state-technocratic rationality (Wright 2010:140–141).

In this model social enterprises could be key components of a reinvigorated and empowered society and not passive recipients of a state largesse and philanthropic goodwill. As democratically-owned and accountable economic entities they would act as locally empowering organisations, and not merely service deliverers, but also represent a new approach to economic and social governance. An approach rooted in solidarity and subsidiarity is also likely to lead to other benefits. For example Richard Wilkinson and Kate Pickett's book *The Spirit Level – Why Equality is Better for Everyone* details how communities that are oriented towards co-operative or social economy models of economic activity tend to be healthier and suffer less from a variety of illnesses (2009:260).

Public Policy Interventions and Unintended Consequences

As noted earlier the debate about the role of social enterprise can often be rooted in distinctly market-based terms and the consequences of this are rarely examined. In the context of the evolving Irish debate it is useful to examine the role of civil society actors in education provision in the United States and the recent changes to the model to facilitate the entry of philanthropic-funded social entrepreneurs. In a recent book, Diane Ravitch, an Assistant Secretary of Education under the 1988-1992 Bush administration, notes the very negative impacts of the charter schools[17] on Catholic schools. In the Irish context it can be difficult to comprehend that Catholic schools can be so separate from the state system of education provision but it is worth noting that they have a very strong record in the United States of providing "a better civic education than many public schools" (Moses 2010:35). Of interest to the debate in Ireland is the long standing, and increasingly successful efforts, by many political activists, supported by a number of large philanthropic foundations, to marketise education. The idea being that schools would flourish if freed from government bureaucracy and punished or rewarded according to their performance. The recent appointment of Betsy DeVos, a key advocate for school choice, school voucher programmes, and charter schools, as US Secretary of Education, is another step in the process of normalisation of previously-regarded fringe ideas.

Ravitch, initially a strong advocate of similar approaches, notes two distinct consequences. First, she finds that schools began to "teach to the test". Students lose out on a more

---

[17] A charter school is a school that receives government funding but operates independently of the established state school system in which it is located. In many cases they are privately owned and their development is seen as an example of public asset privatisation.

rounded education as schools and school districts game the system by changing the grading system, leading to big gains in the number of students passing. In addition she notes the closure of many Catholic schools, rooted in their communities and providing a very good education, because they can't compete with the new providers who are funded by philanthropic foundations like the Bill and Melinda Gates Foundation[18]. Ravitch notes in a chapter entitled "The Billionaire Boys' Club" how philanthropic foundations have a huge influence in American education because of the large amounts of money they've spent to engineer and promote their agenda of business knows best, that schools need to emulate the corporate world by encouraging competition, assessing outcomes, rewarding the success of annual progress in test scores and "firing incompetents" (Moses 2010:35). However as Ravitch observes, "the problem with the marketplace is that it dissolves communities and replaces them with consumers. Going to school is not the same as going shopping" (2010:221).

For Ireland the pertinent lesson is that critically examining the likely consequences of a policy turn to social entrepreneurs is vital, as there is every chance they will undermine existing community-based initiatives, and a reliance on market-based solutions often reflects a complete misunderstanding of the challenge at hand.

A second example directly reflects failings in Irish public policy formulation as it relates to the social economy and the "strange death" of student-owner social enterprises[19]. In the early-mid 1990s Ireland hosted one of the largest student-owned social enterprises in Europe, the Union of Students in Ireland

---

[18] Ravitch notes that the Gates Foundation spend nearly $2 billion on a campaign to close existing schools and replace them with more market-oriented schools before acknowledging that this was a mistake (Ravitch 2010:204-211).

[19] While the Harvard Coop is probably the best known example internationally, student-owned co-operatives had a significant presence in Irish higher education up until quite recently. Due to a variety of factors, primarily the efforts by university and college managements to achieve the maximum short-term gain from their property, social enterprises owned by students have declined dramatically over the course of the past 15 years. They have largely been replaced by externally-owned and managed retail units, usually SPAR or MACE, and bookshops such as Waterstones. The co-operative and mutualist ethos espoused by student-owned enterprises has sadly disappeared and been replaced by a more 'managerial' approach to student needs.

Travel (USIT), and a range of very significant university and college-based organisations, for example DITSU Trading Limited[20]. Unfortunately USIT collapsed due to the undermining of the student aviation market following the 9/11 attacks and the purchase of the US student travel company, CTS, in August 2001[21], and DITSU Trading Limited no longer has a commercial remit due to constraints placed on it by DIT.

The critical issue for student-owned social enterprises was the collapse of the facilitative policy framework or maybe more accurately the development of a policy framework that emphasised short-term commercial returns to universities and colleges. There are two distinct issues in this context. First, the legislative framework for a large number of higher education institutions (HEIs) in Ireland, the Vocational Education Committee Act, 1930, prohibited HEIs from delivering canteen or retail services. This space was filled by student-owned social enterprises. Unfortunately, the successor legislation, the Regional Technical Colleges Act, 1993, and the Dublin Institute of Technology Act, 1993, removed this ban. As a result HEIs could now deliver services themselves.

The second issue was that the state's higher education funding regime forced, and continues to force, HEIs to examine every opportunity to develop alternative sources of income. In this context the rental income provided by retail chains can be a significant annual addition to HEIs' budgets. It is also worth noting that some HEI managements took an unmitigated delight in having an opportunity to undermine student-owned social enterprises[22].

---

[20] This was the trading arm of the Dublin Institute of Technology Students Union. It operated 5 shops, a number of canteens/restaurants and delivered a variety of other services to students of the Institute. It currently does not deliver any commercial services.

[21] In a subsequent legal action by the receiver Mr. Justice Peart said USIT suffered a 'double whammy' after the travel industry suffered due to the 2001 attacks on the US (RTÉ "Court rules on collapse of USIT travel company" 10th August 2005, available at https://www.rte.ie/news/2005/0810/66366-usit/). In essence the company has since been de-mutualised and is now owned by the UK-based Real Experience Group, formerly the Kinlay Group.

[22] The author was a member of the board of directors of DITSU Trading Limited (1992-1998), USIT Supervisory Board (1992-1995), and Seirbhís, the Union of Students in Ireland Commercial Services Company (1992-1997).

In addition, and this relates to the emphasis on the creation of social enterprises that have socialised ownership and control discussed earlier, is the apparent lack of political discourse in the broader student movement that recognises the importance and significant contribution of student-owned social enterprises. As noted above, up until quite recently student-owned social enterprises were common, and provided significant funds to re-invest in student-identified needs, e.g. emergency finance, welfare and medical services. The current perspective appears to be that universities and colleges should provide appropriate services and student collective action, if any, should be focused on charitable fund-raising, for example RAG charities, or individual student social entrepreneurial activity through social mission-oriented organisations. These in turn are often supported by international organisations such as Ashoka or Enactus that only support social mission-type initiatives (Sá and Kretz 2015; Kretz and Sá 2015).

If, as most people would probably accept, a critical aspect of higher education is developing one's sense of citizenship and community, i.e. processes of socialisation, then student-owned social enterprises contribute a great deal to these processes. They develop among students a sense of what is possible and what can be achieved with coherent collective action. In addition, they help create an entrepreneurial spirit within students and they encourage a strong sense of mutualism and community. Surely these remain valid arguments for HEIs to facilitate the establishment/re-establishment of student-owned social enterprises[23].

For the purposes of this chapter the key lesson is that facilitative public policy frameworks are critical success factors for social enterprises and it is very easy to undermine successful ventures with inappropriate or poorly thought through policy interventions. In the context of current discussions about rural

---

[23] For example, students unions, either nationally or locally, could negotiate a leasing-style agreement with HEIs for space for shops etc. and recruit staff familiar with co-operative principles and the ethos of managing a co-operative enterprise. Unlike the Harvard Coop, it is not envisaged that the enterprise would pay an annual dividend to members, rather the annual surplus should be re-invested in the enterprise as had been the case in Irish student-owned social enterprises.

sustainability this is particularly pertinent. There is considerable evidence to suggest that a coherent approach, as it relates to public policy, to the social economy in rural areas can provide significant social and economic dividends (Steinerowski and Steinerowska-Streb 2012; Zografos 2007; Eversole *et al.* 2014). The challenge is devising the appropriate policy framework rather than facilitating piecemeal financial interventions.

Questioning the Role of Social Enterprise and Social Entrepreneurs

An objective of this chapter was to contribute to an ongoing debate in the broad social economy, in which both social enterprises and social entrepreneurs operate, particularly as the current political and economic environment appears to be conducive to a major reconfiguring of Irish economic activity in favour of the social economy. However it is unclear what the many actors in the Irish social economy are striving for. Is there a shared vision? Given the different origins, backgrounds and objectives of the many organisations and individuals, is such a suggestion even possible? The confusing jumble of terms, e.g. social innovation, social economy, social enterprise, community and voluntary sectors, social entrepreneurs etc., is striking. The fact that each term has a different meaning to different people is equally telling and clearly indicates not only the lack of a shared vision but also the absence of a shared vocabulary. Furthermore it is telling that most political parties have no policy stances in this area[24].

In this context it is helpful to discuss 'developmental' and 'instrumental' perspectives on social enterprise and social entrepreneurs. From the developmental perspective, there is an intrinsic and empowering value in the growth of the social economy in Ireland. From the instrumental perspective, i.e. as a means to another end, and it appears that some in the Irish government share this perspective, it is the efficiency gains that

_____

[24] With the exception of the Social Democrats, who developed a policy on community banking (see https://socialdemocrats.ie/policies/create-community-banking-sector/ for details) and Sinn Féin, who developed a policy on social clauses in public procurement contracts (see http://www.sinnfein.ie/files/2015/PublicProcurementDoc_2015.pdf for details).

flow from the application of business principles by social entrepreneurs that make social enterprises useful or worthwhile. By delivering certain services cheaper and more effectively they serve an important purpose. Neither of these perspectives is to be condemned or lauded, they are rooted in political and ideological perspectives, but they are different and, while not mutually exclusive, the policy interventions necessary to facilitate either or both are distinct. Michael Edwards warns that the social economy "needs different organising principles from business because it has different goals" (2009:9). That doesn't mean inefficiency is somehow inherent to the social economy. It just means its goals are different and sometimes policy makers forget to remember that and focus on relatively obscure problems such as displacement, i.e. how many jobs will be lost in the private sector (real jobs) as the social economy expands because for many policy makers and politicians only the market creates real jobs.

Conclusion
In most European states democratisation and the rise of the modern welfare state provided the foundation for "unprecedented improvements in the material conditions of the bulk of society, and greater room for the actualisation of individuals' skills, aptitudes and talents" (Wood and Roper 2004:253). Ireland had a rather unusual trajectory, at least in relation to other EU member states, and social enterprises have played a very significant role in our societal development, particularly in rural Ireland, e.g. Raiffiesen Banks[25], Approved Local Councils[26], Credit Unions and Agricultural Co-operatives, and the current economic crises have provided an opportunity for many to question the role of the state in providing certain services. That is fair and appropriate. It is not necessarily regressive and doesn't amount to an attack on the 'public sphere'. It is possible to envision an alternative model of development that is empowering, committed to social justice

---

[25] Raiffeisen Banks operated in Ireland from the 1890s until the early 1930s (Colvin and McLoughlin 2012).
[26] Approved Local Councils operated in a number of Irish communities in the 1940s and 1950s and delivered services on behalf of county councils (Gallagher 2000).

and a redistributive capitalism and not wedded to what GDH Cole called the "omnicompetent state" (1920:2).

However, the language employed by many writers about social entrepreneurs, and by social entrepreneurs themselves is problematic. It appears to take for granted that the state, and for that matter any form of co-ordinated public action, is inherently inefficient and needs to be marketised. That somehow the application of business processes will address complex social and economic problems. The consequences of this ideological action remain largely unquestioned. Why? Given the possibilities for the provision of social and infrastructural services on offer there is a danger that an approach to the social economy may be adopted and implemented by the Irish state that is socially unsustainable, i.e. rather than invest in the social and community infrastructure necessary to develop and sustain an expanding social economy there may be a trend to outsource the delivery of services to community-based organisations that are not equipped to manage a significant increase in turnover or support for socially unsustainable social entrepreneurs.

It is both essential and feasible to embed the social economy as a key component of a model of economic development in Ireland and this process has to be embedded in a robust series of discussions about the role and nature of the social economy and relative roles of social innovation, social enterprise and social entrepreneurs, how they see themselves, how others perceive them and how a consensus might be developed. At this stage in Ireland's social and economic development it is vital we avoid what Roberto Unger refers to as the "dictatorship of no alternatives" (2009:1).

SECTION II
ECOSYSTEMS

CHAPTER 5
PUBLIC INVESTMENT IN SOCIAL INNOVATION IN IRELAND: A CASE STUDY OF SOCIAL INNOVATION FUND IRELAND

Deirdre Mortell

Introduction

Everyone in Ireland knows someone affected by dementia; urban or rural, young or old, it touches us all. Finding the right care for our loved ones can be challenging no matter where we live. In rural areas, it is most challenging of all. Carebright Village in Bruff, County Limerick has set out to develop the first dementia-friendly housing project, especially for people living in rural areas. It is based on a community model in the Netherlands. It is now built, and residents will move in by the end of 2017. They hope this will be a model for dementia-friendly housing for rural communities across Ireland.

Early school leaving is a hidden problem in Ireland; 3,600 young people leave school every year before Junior Certificate, that's 10 per day. iScoil in Dublin has developed an online learning programme that enables young people to learn at home, regardless of whether they have been excluded from school or cannot attend due to mental health issues or social phobias. iScoil combines technology, personal learning plans, trained mentors and subject tutors, all offered online, to enable young people to get a Junior Certificate (at least), without attending school. iScoil plans to grow from its current 50 students per year to 250 students over a number of years. The demand is even greater.

These are just two examples of social innovations backed by Social Innovation Fund Ireland in 2016. This chapter will outline the origins and development of the Social Innovation Fund, share some examples of the funds work and reflect on the challenges to and opportunities for social innovation into the future.

Public Investment in Social Innovation: A Case Study of Social Innovation Fund Ireland

Social Innovation Fund Ireland's (SIFI) mission is to provide growth capital and supports to the best social innovations in Ireland, to enable them to scale and maximise their impact. Our vision is that Ireland will have the world's best system for supporting social innovation. SIFI defines 'social innovation' as any solution to a critical social issue in Ireland, that is innovative in the context of Ireland. We wish to back those social innovations that are scalable or replicable and that want to grow. We limit our backing to those which are based on the island of Ireland, and which are not for profit[27].

We believe that communities, organisations and individuals in Ireland are constantly evolving and inventing innovative solutions to social and environmental issues that affect them. However, we also believe that these solutions rarely spread from one community to another. The issues that we face in Ireland – homelessness, the impacts of climate change, inequality, an ageing population, youth under-employment, and so many more – are urgent enough that we can't wait for each community to re-invent the wheel. SIFI sets out to find and back the best solutions to various issues, and help them to grow and spread.

SIFI is the venture capital fund for the social innovation sector. We use the tools and methodologies of venture capital, combined with growth capital structured as grants, to back the best social innovations we can find that match our criteria. Fundamentally our tools and methodologies are the non-financial supports (that we know from business) needed to grow innovative models. SIFI varies these inputs based on the issue being addressed and the stage of development of the initiative. They include; appointment of an experienced volunteer mentor; appointment of a consultant to support growth planning, business modelling and/or financial modelling; technical

---

[27] Grantees must have a non-profit legal form, which is defined by having 3 specific clauses in its governing articles – an asset lock ensuring that in the event of its winding up, the assets are applied to a similar purpose, and any profit or surplus, must be re-invested in the mission, rather than distributed to Members or others, by way of fees, bonus or other. No Officer of the organisation may receive any remuneration or benefit.

supports; access to a peer problem solving network; and access to SIFI networks. A portfolio manager is also appointed to work with the grantee during the lifetime of the grant; managing the relationship and coordinating the inputs.

SIFI grant payments are performance-based and are typically structured with 30-50% paid up front on selection. The balance is paid subject to meeting performance milestones. These milestones are agreed with the grantee on selection and form part of the funding contract. Payments can be delayed by SIFI until milestones are met.

SIFI is funded through a public-private partnership model. SIFI raises private philanthropic funds, and each euro of this is matched by a euro from Government. The source of these funds is the Dormant Accounts Fund, which are channelled to SIFI through the Department of Rural and Community Development[28]. The mechanism requires SIFI to evidence the philanthropic funds in writing, in order to draw down the match funding, which as a result, is a lag funding model. No other government funds are provided so SIFI is required to fund its own operations through a charge to match funds. SIFI is an independent company and charity. In its opening phase, the minister at the time nominated a company member and a director. When these terms are completed there are no further nominations built into the governing instruments. As a result SIFI operates at arm's length from the Irish Government.

Origins of the Social Innovation Fund

Social Innovation Fund Ireland defines social innovation as any innovative solution to a criticial social issue in Ireland. A more sophisticated but also more complex definition could be "a social innovation is a novel solution to a social problem that is more effective, efficient, sustainable, or just than current solutions. The value created accrues primarily to society rather than to private individuals" (Phills, Deiglmeier, and Miller, 2008:39) Other definitions are broader, including social

---

[28] SIFI funding has been channelled through various Departments since 2014, including the Department of Housing, Planning and Local Government (2016 - mid 2017), Department of Environment, Community and Local Government (2014-16), and the (new) Department of Rural & Community Development from July 2017.

innovation as a process, not just a solution or product. As Innovate Dublin (2017) states "Social innovations can also spread in the form of ideas, values, software, tools and habits". All of these definitions are valid and should not be seen as mutually exclusive.

SIFI was formed as a result of a recommendation of the Forum on Philanthropy and Fundraising, which was appointed by Phil Hogan TD, Minister for Environment, Community and Local Government in 2011. This forum, chaired by Frank Flannery, had a brief to find ways to stimulate philanthropy in the context of the closure of the two largest grant making foundations in Ireland, both of which supported social issues. Atlantic Philanthropies and ONE Foundation[29] were both due to cease grant making between 2013-2016. The Report on the Forum on Philanthropy and Fundrasing (2011:24) outlined that this would leave "an annual €60m gulf in funding for the Irish social sector. It is now imperative that new philanthropists are found and new foundations established to fill this vacuum, with potentially disastrous effects on support for social causes in Ireland". The recommendations contained within this report were adopted by An Taoiseach Enda Kenny TD and the report was launched in July 2012. The report stated:

> The Forum recommends the creation of a Social Innovation Fund of a significant size (starting at €10m+) to support the establishment and growth of social innovations with the potential for transformative impact on critical social issues facing Ireland, including unemployment and the environment (Forum on Philanthropy and Fundraising, 2011:4).

It concluded

> The Forum's vision for the period 2011-2016 is that the role and legitimacy of the contribution of philanthropy and strategic charitable fundraising to Irish society

---

[29] I was CEO of ONE Foundation for its ten year life 2004 – 2013.

will be reinforced, properly understood and valued
(Forum on Philanthropy and Fundraising, 2011: 4).

Following the report's adoption by Cabinet, *Social Innovation Fund Ireland* was registered as a company in 2013, at the request of the Minister for the Environment, Community and Local Government at that time, Phil Hogan TD, and commenced operations in late 2014, following receipt of a funding contract from this Department. Unusually, as a result, SIFI has a dual mission – to stimulate philanthropy and so increase the amount of philanthropic giving in Ireland, and, also, to back social innovations that can scale and spread. These operate as two sides of the same coin.

SIFI's early intentions were to back a range of models in order to demonstrate both the impact, but also the variety of social innovation solutions that were present in Ireland or could be created with the right conditions in place. These include, for example, social service solutions that fill gaps in the market or where the market is not viable, such as eldercare or childcare in rural or disadvantaged areas. The Animate 2016 Awardee Carebright Village, mentioned earlier, is an example of such an initiative.

We also sought to back data or technology-driven solutions which needed early or growth stage support. The THINKTECH awardees including iScoil are examples of this. Finally, disruptive solutions to issues can emerge. Animate 2016 Awardee *Save a Selfie* (now EMAIN), identified the lack of a national database of defribillators which placed lives at risk as they could not be located in an emergency. It uses mapping technology to crowdsource their locations, creating an online open data set of defibrillator locations (they are usually privately owned by employers or sports clubs). The next stage of this initiative will build the database to monitor battery life and maintenance records to ensure that they are always functional.

Why was Government drawn to the Public Investment Model?
A review of international models by the Forum on Philanthropy and Fundraising revealed that many OECD countries had a vehicle to support innovative solutions to key social issues that was initiated and at least part funded by government. The

models varied depending on who operated them – government or independent, or a hybrid of both. The funding model also varied; endowment funded, match funded only, or both. Ireland had no vehicle to back social innovation at this time, and the Social Innovation Fund Ireland model was born. The Forum report stated

> Social Innovation Funds have a strong track record internationally. In the first half of 2010, £3.7m of government investment in Inspiring Scotland was leveraged by philanthropy to bring 1,311 young NEETs (Not in Education, Employment, or Training) back into economic activity. Between 2003 and 2009, the Serbian Social Innovation Fund has transformed social services, increasing the coverage of social care services from 12 to 100 municipalities with €7m of national funding. In America in 2010, the i3 fund secured $140m of private investment to increase the levels of educational attainment in American public schools, while the Social Innovation Fund allowed government to triple a $50m investment in high-performance not-for-profits" (Forum on Philanthropy and Fundraising, 2011:24).

The proposed model was based on a combination of two others. The American Social Innovation Fund was created during President Obama's first hundred days in office in 2009, as a delivery of his presidential campaign promise. It operates within the White House, as part of the Corporation for National Service, and as such it is federally funded, for core funds and grant funds. The U.S. Social Innovation Fund demands leverage of $3 for every $1 that it invests in grant funding to selected programmes. These funds are focused on scaling programmes that meet specific policy objectives of the Administration with the simple but vital goal of

> finding what works, and making it work for more people, the Social Innovation Fund and its grantees create a learning network of organizations working to implement innovative and effective evidence-based solutions to local and national challenges in three

priority areas: economic opportunity, healthy futures, and youth development.

Social Innovation Fund is a powerful approach to transforming lives and communities that positions the federal government to be a catalyst for impact— mobilizing private resources to find and grow community solutions with evidence of results (Corporation of National and Community Service 2017).

Importantly, the fund is focused on tightly defined policy issues, and it aims to scale and spread solutions that work[30]. Minister Hogan TD had the opportunity to interrogate this model during a meeting with Paul Carttar, former CEO of the American Social Innovation Fund, in Dublin in 2012.

The second model to inform the SIFI model was that of Inspiring Scotland. Inspiring Scotland had been created as a joint venture of the Scottish Government and Lloyds TSB Foundation in 2006, with the aim of supporting and growing effective programmes that supported young people known as NEETs (Not in Education, Employment or Training) back onto a path with hope and potential for a future.

Both of these very different organisations were started by their respective governments and had; public/private partnership at the heart of their funding models, a mission to grow and scale proven effective solutions to social issues that formed part of key policy objectives for their governments, and used grants and non-financial supports to deliver this growth.

These common elements also formed the core of the SIFI model – both funding and investment. The decision by Government to create SIFI using this model, could be viewed as aligning with standard OECD practice by governments, rather than as a fundamentally new departure. Choosing to use Dormant Accounts Funds to provide the (match) funding, significantly de-risked the political decision to create this new initiative. Dormant Accounts Funds are controlled by Government, but they are funded from unused bank deposits,

---

[30] Social Innovation Fund was quietly de-funded by the Trump Administration earlier in 2017.

not by tax revenues, and as such they are not tax payers' money. Their purpose is defined in legislation[31] and is highly aligned with SIFI mission, as it requires funds to be spent on innovation that tackles socio-economic disadvantage, educational disadvantage, or the effects of disability. Section 41 (1) (a) of the Dormant Accounts Act (2000) states

> The moneys in the investment and disbursements account shall be applied by the Agency, on the direction of the Board, for the following purposes: programmes or projects that are designed to assist the personal, educational and social development of persons who are economically, educationally or socially disadvantaged or persons with a disability (within the meaning of the Equal Status Act 2000) and, in particular, programmes or projects that are designed to assist primary school students with learning difficulties.

It is important to recall that in 2012 Ireland was in the grip of austerity budgets, and the creation of new initiatives was almost politically and financially impossible.

Social Innovation Fund Ireland - Selection Process and Criteria
SIFI has six core selection criteria which grantees must meet. Successful projects must tackle a critical social issue (giving evidence as to why they believe that the issue they address is a critical one) and they must offer a solution that is innovative in the context of other solutions available in Ireland. SIFI must be convinced that the solution is scalable or replicable in Ireland. Additionally, it must be not for profit, based on the island of Ireland, and have the potential to make impact in Ireland.

Additional criteria will depend on the various calls for applications for solutions to address specific issues. For example SIFI's 'Education Fund' called for innovative programmes that provide qualifications to traditional early school leavers within the field of education. SIFI may also call for projects at a specific

---

[31] Dormant Accounts Act (2001).

stage of development, for example the Animate programme calls for early stage projects.

SIFI's selection process is robust and draws on experts and non-experts as part of the selection process. All SIFI funds are opened by a public call for applications which is open for a minimum of four weeks and which is promoted widely within Ireland through social media, grassroots activation, SIFI's network and wider non-profit networks. In some cases SIFI have embarked on a roadshow around the country. The application process is a simple one. Forms are completed online and free of charge. In order to allow applicants with more limited writing skills to make a strong application they can also make a short video (on a smart phone or tablet).

There are six stages in the process. Stage one eliminates the applications that patently do not meet the criteria e.g. those with no impact in Ireland. Stage two screens the applications. Applications are sent to independent volunteers to read and apply the SIFI criteria. Feedback is provided in a structured way with each application categorised as 'strong', 'potential' or 'weak'. The 'screeners' come from a wide range of backgrounds, and their function is advisory only. SIFI staff also read all applications at this stage, and apply the same process. All applications are read by at least two people. Based on the recommedations of the screening process a selection of applicants are invited for interview. They are typically from the 'strong' and 'potential' categories. Stage three is the interview process. SIFI recruits interview panels from business, government agency and social sector leaders, as well as SIFI staff, to interview applicants. Interview questions are informed by feedback from the screening stage. Interview panels, which are advisory only, are asked to reach a joint recommendation of 'strong', 'potential' or 'weak'. Due diligence is carried out in stage four. SIFI verifies nonprofit status, financial stability, and governance. SIFI also verifies programmatic claims through references and considers the timing and the ability of the applicant to benefit from the non-financial elements of the award. In the fifth stage SIFI staff consider the recommendations, results of due diligence, and examine the finalists as a portfolio (taking into account the need to ensure diversity). They then recommend a portfolio of applicants to the

SIFI Board. The sixth and final stage is the SIFI board make the final decision.

What has Social Innovation Fund Achieved So Far?

At three years old SIFI has met its founding challenge from Government which was to raise €5 million in philanthropic funds, thus creating a €10 million social innovation fund. To date SIFI has raised €5.15 million in pledged philanthropic funds which are eligible to be matched by government, and drawn down €2.2 million in matching funds. These philanthropic funds are donated and pledged by a wide range of donors – multinational companies, indigenous Irish companies, as well as individuals, families and small and medium sized businesses, and trusts. This has been achieved despite the fact that, although a registered charity, SIFI does not yet offer tax effective giving to donors[32]. Five calls for applications have been opened in that time, with a portfolio of 31 awardees selected to date.

Animate was the first 'fund' opened, in 2015, offering €80,000 in grants and accelerator supports to any early stage solution to a critical social issue. Four awardees were selected – *Recreate, Thriftify, Save a Selfie* and *Carebright Village*. They were offered up to €10,000 in a cash grant, plus a budget of equal value to be used for growth planning, mentoring, and a specially designed 'Growth Training Programme' a day a month for five months. Collectively these are the 'accelerator supports referred to below.

SIFI's second fund THINKTECH is Ireland's first TechForGood Fund. It was created by SIFI in collaboration with Google.org and the government in 2016. Its purpose is to support ideas for a better Ireland with technology and innovation at their core. A donation of €500,000 by Google.org, matched by the government, created a fund of €750,000 for 3-4 awardees to share. Four awardees were selected – *Foodcloud Hubs, iScoil, The Alone Platform* (a collaboration of Alone and Netwell Casala), and a special early stage award for *Space Engagers*. Growth stage awardees received €160,000 to €170,000

---

[32] The Revenue Commissioners require a probation period of 2 years before newly registered charities can offer tax effective giving to donors. SIFI will qualify in December 2017.

in cash grants plus a budget of €50,000 in accelerator supports, including growth planning, mentoring, technical supports, and an Accelerator programme of a day per month for five months. The early stage award was €100,000.

The Education Fund was opened later in 2016 to test a new model of backing social innovation. Applicants are required to meet educational criteria relating to innovative solutions to achieving qualifications for early school leavers at QQI levels 3-6. Additionally, and for the first time, they are given the opportunity to raise their own donor funds of €10,000 or more over one year or more (with no upper limit). SIFI can then provide 'uplift' funds. Awardees additionally receive accelerator supports such as an external evaluation of their programme, which are funded from the 'uplift funds'. Ten very diverse awardees were selected with programmes targeting adult and young early school leavers, including ex-prisoners, homeless men, out-of-school young people, and DEIS second level schools. Funds raised by awardees range from €45,000 to over €1 million. Donors are as diverse as awardees – individuals, families, small and medium sized companies, large companies, and trusts.

SIFI's fourth fund, Engage & Educate, was opened in 2017 and focuses on community-based education initiatives. The fund amounts to €450,000 over three years. Four projects share the 2017 fund of €150,000. Awardees tackle the barriers to education found in; experiencing mental health issues, by being a migrant, by being a DEIS primary school student, and by having an intellectual disability. Engage & Educate is supported through a partnership between SIFI and leading law firm Mason Hayes & Curran, which has a long serving commitment to access to education.

The Animate Fund opened for the second time in June 2017 with an increased number of awards available. Ten are focused on healthy community initiatives, and supported by Medtronic Foundation, and one award is open to any early stage solution to a critical social issue.

The Resilient Communities Fund opened in October 2017. It seeks projects that build communities that are economically, socially or environmentally resilient and that are scalable or replicable in Ireland. It is supported by the Cork-based Tomar Trust.

SIFI's next planned fund will focus on social enterprise development.

SIFI has ambitious plans for 2017 and the future. We are proud that we have secured over €5 million in philanthropic funds to date. We have begun a trajectory that will see us raising significantly more philanthropic funds year on year, seeking out innovations that accelerate our ability to solve social issues. These innovations may be new models of care or new financial models. We will communicate with policy makers with regard to what is needed to assist in the spreading and scaling of initiatives in urban and rural settings. We will share our learning through traditional and social media. We will also seek to lead a national conversation, through traditional media, social and digital media as well as grassroots work, on the role that social innovation can play in our nation's future. Finally, we will work to connect further with existing networks in rural areas and towns, and with the counties where we have seen fewer applications to the fund to date.

How can we Measure the Impact of SIFI and What is the Potential to Create Impact in Supporting and Growing Social Innovation in Ireland?

SIFI aims to measure its impact in two ways, just as its mission is like two sides of the same coin – stimulating philanthropy and supporting social innovation. Philanthropy stimulation is measured by the size of the philanthropic funds raised by SIFI. To date, SIFI has raised committed funds of €5.1 million in its first three years. Measuring the social impact of Social Innovation Fund Ireland is of course a much more difficult task, which will always remain a work in progress. During the opening three years, SIFI has been able to capture quantitative and qualitative measures of impact. Quantitative measures include jobs created and next stage funds raised. Project level outputs can also be measured which are unique to each project. Qualitative measures to date include perceptions of the impact of the programme on the project's progress (e.g. testimonials), and ranking of the various programme elements to capture the learning in each programme's design.

Social Innovation Fund Ireland is committed to being a learning organisation and feedback, anonymous and otherwise, is captured throughout each programme, from awardees, mentors, and consultants. SIFI is also committed to operating to, and perhaps leading, international standards and so draws regularly from international peers in the social innovation field. Capturing the full impact of SIFI and scaling and spreading social innovations and their impact around Ireland is a long-term project which is just beginning.

Social innovation has always existed in Ireland, in so far as individuals, communities, and organisations, both state and private sector, have always innovated to find or create solutions to Ireland's social issues, both new and entrenched. What is new is that the language of social innovation is being used by early adopters, some creating new work, such as Innovate Dublin, and some applying the term to existing work. This is not inherently problematic. The term 'social innovation' can act as a brand to draw attention and resources to existing innovative initiatives which did not meet the parameters for support before the arrival of this new category 'social innovation'. Thus, social innovation as a formal construct remains a very new concept in Ireland, driven mainly by developments (and funding) from the European Commission.

Some commentators identify confusion between 'social innovation', 'social enterprise' and 'social entrepreneurship', all relatively new terms. Social innovation is focused on the idea. Social enterprise is focused on the business model, which requires at least some trading revenues (UK definition sets this at minimum 30% of income). Social entrepreneurship is focused on the person or leader, who must have entrepreneurial skills or traits.

Social enterprise and social innovation have their roots in Europe, whereas social entrepreneurship has its roots in North America driven by organisations such as Ashoka[33], and adopted later by Social Entrepreneurs Ireland, by UnLtd in the UK, and Ferd Social Entrepreneurs in Norway. It can be argued that social enterprise has its roots in the cooperative movement, with

---

[33] Ashoka was created by Bill Drayton in USA in 1982 to spread the seeds of social entrepreneurship. It is now a global organisation.

a long tradition in continental Europe as well as in Ireland and UK.

In Ireland today, there is some evidence that rural and urban social enterprises display very different characteristics and play very different roles in their communities. Rural social enterprises are often focused on social service provision, through a strong community base, for example Carebright provides home help to older people in rural areas in Cork, Kerry and Limerick. Fort Dunree in Inishowen, County Donegal, Camden Fort in Crosshaven, County Cork and UNESCO accredited Copper Coast Geopark in Waterford are all examples of tourism initiatives. Urban social enterprises are more likely to be focused on employment creation or training for long term unemployed people, for example Ecomattress, a mattress recycling project in Dublin city, or Meitheal Mara, which provides boat building training, in Cork City.

Funding for social enterprise has emerged from different sources at different times. The European Social Fund (ESF) provided significant grant funds in the 1980s and 1990s for social enterprises focused on employment training. This European funding enabled the establishment of Rehab Group. In more recent years, grant funds for social enterprise of circa €1 million per year have been provided from the Irish Government through Pobal. Grant funding for social enterprise has also been available from the European Union through INTERREG and LEADER programmes.

The Social Inclusion Community Activation Programme (SICAP) has also added social enterprise to the projects which it can support. The Social Finance Foundation in Ireland is a wholesaler of loan funding to social enterprises via retail loan providers Clann Credo and Community Finance Ireland. Their clients have traditionally been rurally based, but the evidence suggests that this is changing. The Social Finance Foundation has been able to leverage its funds through the European Union's Employment and Social Innovation Fund Programme (EaSI) which seeks to reduce the risk of providing loan finance to social enterprises.

Social entrepreneurship in Ireland is funded almost exclusively through private philanthropy. The European Investment Fund (EIF) offers finance through its Social

Entrepreneurs Fund, but to my knowledge it has not yet been drawn down in Ireland.

To achieve funding of social innovation at scale we will need to crack the issue of demonstrating and proving impact. This requires much greater engagement between universities, economists, social innovators, and policy makers in order to reach a determination of what counts as impact. Quantifiable impact is relatively easy to measure, but qualitative impact is arguably more important and of course much more difficult to establish with rigour. Let us take for example the impact of social housing schemes which aims to house homeless families. How do we balance addressing urgent and immediate issues with achieving a longer term objective? It is easy to count the number of families housed but do they have to be already homeless to be counted? Should social housing be targeted first at families who are already homeless or those that are at the top of the housing list – sometimes for up to ten years. How should the system prioritise between homeless families and families at risk of homelessness? Housing policy clearly states that mixed housing is desirable – in this case, should the system house those not at risk of homelessness ahead of those who are in order to meet the long-term policy goals? Should the state ask a homeless family with complex needs to wait longer for supported housing services that will meet their needs more fully in the future? How can the qualitative impact over time of housing (or not) a child or young person be captured. i.e. the impact of moving schools, the absence of a quiet space to do homework, being alienated or exhausted at school, family stress and being separated from extended family, friends, and pets. These all have an impact on educational outcomes.

Open data on the costs and outcomes of existing state and other services is rare in Ireland making it difficult to demonstrate the effectiveness and value for money of an innovation. Until we can devise clear research methodologies to capture impact, that also enable value for money analysis, we will struggle to demonstrate the value of social innovation in tackling wicked problems like homelessness or mental health issues.

Opportunities

The importance of social innovation in Ireland will grow dramatically in the coming years. The focus of policymaking and funding in the areas of employment creation focused on social enterprise; and social problem solving focused on social innovation, (with a special focus on employment and training for long term unemployed people, young people, and migrants, on social inclusion, and on building sustainable rural communities) from the European Commission will drive this. Increasing the Irish Government matched funding to €50 million to create a potential €100 million fund through SIFI will dramatically scale up the funds available to support social innovation in a way that is flexible and responsive to local issues throughout Ireland.

However, Ireland is substantially underdeveloped relative to our usual comparators (Scotland and England). We are closer aligned to Portugal in this regard. Social Innovation Fund Ireland was created by Government in 2013 to address this. We are now, in partnership with companies, universities, government, and social innovators building momentum. There is evidence of a growing movement of champions for innovation in solving social issues. These include business leaders, policymakers, politicians, social innovators, academics and young people.

The role of innovation in developing a strong economy and the role of social innovation in solving social issues will be better understood over time. Supporting social innovation is at the heart of the European Commission's strategy for Europe to 2020, as evidenced in the following statement

> The EESC considers that social enterprises should be supported by virtue of the key role that they can play as drivers of social innovation, both because they introduce new methods for providing services and measures aimed at improving people's quality of life, and because they promote the creation of new products to satisfy society's new needs (European Economic and Social Committee of the European Parliament 2012:1).

The Irish Government's Programme for a Partnership Government, pledges to increase the match funding available to SIFI to €50 million from its current level of €5 million. This will create a potential social innovation fund of €100 million providing opportunities to increase funding to the Irish social innovation scene.

The number of political champions for social innovation is growing. SIFI has engaged with a wide range of cabinet ministers including An Taoiseach Leo Varadkar TD, former Taoiseach Enda Kenny TD, Minister Simon Coveney TD (now Minister for Foreign Affairs and Trade), Minister Paschal Donohoe TD (now Minister for Finance), Minister for Education and Skills Richard Bruton TD, Minister Eoghan Murphy TD (Minister for Housing), plus Ministers of State Dara Murphy TD and John Halligan TD. Young Social Innovators have successfully engaged senior politicians of all political views for many years. However it is questionable as to whether they recall the social innovations or the young people's charisma and energy.

The North South Social Innovation Network has been established by academic institutions on both sides of the border. Brexit presents a considerable threat to its development, right from the start. Trinity College Dublin's Business School has won €12 million in Horizon 2020 funding for a social innovation network of nature-based businesses across European cities, from Malaga to Vienna to Dublin[34]. However, research and data on social innovation in Ireland remains almost non-existent, with the effect that practitioners are relied on to provide a profile of the sector's activities and trends, wth a proliferation of verbal information, which is difficult to substantiate. We need research, stories, champions, funds, political commitment, leadership, social innovators. Does it sound like too much? Social innovation is an early stage field, so it will take what it takes for any early stage field to develop. We have done it before in Ireland, and we can do it again. To conclude I will set out a few ideas on what specifically will be needed and can make a difference.

---

[34] More details about this initiative are available at http://www.connectingnature.eu/

Establishing a Research Agenda

The lack of both quantitative data and case studies is a huge challenge to the communication of social innovation to policymakers, media and communities. Increased academic and practitioner research is a key requirement to deliver this potential. The basis of the research agenda should include the scale of social innovation, trend data, regional data, comparative data to international studies, both European and global. Research should also ask the following questions – which issues are most prominent, why and in which regions? What patterns can we discern as to who leads? How is impact measured? What can we learn? What can we export? Where can Ireland lead?

Bamboozled by Definitions

There are many definitions for social innovation, and we agree with them all. The issue is not definition it is action. We must stop arguing about definitions, and embrace what we have in common, and what we can build together. Social enterprise, social innovation and social entrepreneurship will always overlap, and are intrinsically linked. Ireland needs more of all of them.

Moving from Bursts of Energy to Sustained Social Impact

We have clusters of activity, such as in Ballyhoura on the Cork / Limerick border, and bursts of energy, but we do not yet have sustained activity which can bring about clear social impact and defined social value. Our closest example of sustained impact is Young Social Innovators which has been backing initiatives and programmes with young people for more than ten years. But we cannot place the responsibility for solving our social issues on our second level students, talented and committed as they are.

Most of all it will take collaboration. We must break down the silos between academia and practitioners, between business innovation and social innovation, between business and social investors. Are there signs of hope? I am Social Entrepreneur in Residence, and SIFI is embedded in CONNECT, a Science Foundation Ireland telecommunications research centre based at Trinity College Dublin and linking nine other third level research institutions on the island, with the aim of ensuring that the impact of telecommunications research has positive social as well as economic outcomes. This was made possible by CONNECT's visionary leader Professor Linda Doyle as well as Science Foundation Ireland's growing focus on social as well as economic impact. This model of a Social Entrepreneur in Residence is a first for a SFI research centre and the impact we can deliver together is still emerging. Collaboration is hard but it is the only way forward. We are a small country with a population the size of Manchester, we all speak the same language, and surely we can step up to do this?

A policy agenda
Placing social innovation and social enterprise at the heart of social and economic policy would be a great start. The recent political commitment to a new social enterprise strategy in 2017 is an important step Delivering the Programme for Government commitment to develop a potential €100 million fund for social innovation in 2017-18 is critical.

Getting beyond philanthropy
Stimulating the social investment market to enable private investment in social enterprises and social businesses could look like several things. Creating a legal vehicle to enable this, drawing from international experience and legal models, such as the Community Interest Company (CIC) in the UK or the BCorps entity in USA, would enable social enterprises to access private investment funds and significantly assist them to scale. For example, some social services such as social and affordable housing or nursing home services would naturally lend themselves to a social enterprise model but they cannot do so because they are too capital intensive,. This development would enable Ireland to respond to wicked problems like the challenges of ageing or the housing crisis with private and public support, while providing quality local employment in Ireland. There will always be more private investment than philanthropic investment available. Enabling social innovation at all stages to access capital from start up through growth would significantly accelerate the ability to scale social innovations that are proven to work.

Ireland has demonstrated through its recent management of, and exit from its austerity programme enforced by the troika, that it can act decisively, coordinating all arms of policy and government when it chooses to do so. This is an opportunity to do so again, leveraging our mid-point location between Boston and Berlin.

CHAPTER 6
SOCIAL INNOVATION AND THE COMMUNITY, VOLUNTARY AND CHARITY SECTOR

Deirdre Garvey

Introduction

The purpose of this chapter is to explore the role of social innovation in the Irish community, voluntary and charity sector. It examines how prevalent it is as well as how and where it is taking place within the field. I will also propose what the key actors can do to foster progress and promote social innovation in the sector.

The Wheel is Ireland's national association of community, voluntary and charitable organisations, with over 1,300 member organisations. It is unique in its role as a 'one-stop shop' for anything related to the charity sector. Through the size and diversity of The Wheel's membership, it reaches the invisible infrastructure of Irish society.

The Wheel passionately believes that people, through their participation in community, voluntary and charity organisations, play a central role in improving and enriching life in Ireland. Our simple yet ambitious mission is to help make Ireland a more fair and just place for all by strengthening the capacity and capability of these organisations. We represent the sector's shared interests to government, to other decision-makers and to the media, and we work to promote a better understanding by the public of Irish charities and community organisations and their impacts. In short, we work to ensure that the sector is recognised and respected, adequately resourced and proportionally regulated.

The Wheel builds networks of interest, shares learnings, provides information and delivers essential training on a host of relevant topics. We are enthusiastically committed to transparency, accountability and high standards of practice and governance for our members, the community, voluntary and charity sector, and ourselves. Our core belief is that people, through their active participation in the work of community and voluntary organisations, play a critical and effective role in improving and enriching life in Ireland. We believe that a strong, vibrant, independent and autonomous community and voluntary sector is critically important for sustaining a fair and just society and a healthy democracy.

Social innovation is at the heart of what the community, voluntary and charitable sector is about in Ireland, and in my role as CEO of The Wheel, I lead an organisation that is concerned with helping our members, and the wider sector, to maximise social innovation in their work.

Social Innovation and the Community, Voluntary and Charitable Sector

Social innovation is the development of novel solutions to particular problems. It requires openness to learning, a willingness to scan the environment for new ideas and to take calculated risks. The community, voluntary and charity sector has always been an engine for social innovation in Ireland. However, the sector can play an even more significant role in promoting social innovation if community, voluntary and charitable organisations challenge their attitudes to innovation, and government puts supports in place to foster innovative practice.

Ireland today is a world away from anything our forebears could have imagined. Likewise, it will likely be a very different place again in a few decades time. Many unforeseen challenges have arisen throughout our history and so many more will arise in the coming years. Ireland has adapted and will continue to adapt. Over the past number of decades new challenges have emerged – globalisation, largescale migration, climate change and an ageing population, to name just a few - all set against a backdrop of profound economic change. Moreover, global terror threats are compounding the prevailing sense of insecurity.

This places a duty on organised civil society to respond and adapt to emerging challenges by offering new solutions to new problems and exploring new ways to tackle unforeseen challenges. Social innovation can and does make a real difference in meeting these issues head on, and it offers fresh and dynamic approaches to mobilising communities and increasing their resilience. Often the very best solutions come from ordinary people who, living in their own communities, are facing specific problems and who in turn collectively respond with innovative ideas and creativity. Necessity is indeed the mother of invention.

Social innovation happens around us every day. We do it without realising it: from car-pooling to educating our children in new and different ways – the example of Educate Together schools springs to mind - or the growing Fair Trade movement. We see it all around us, but we often do not recognise it as social innovation *per se*.

When the community and voluntary sector works well, it demonstrates its abilities in these areas (social innovation characterises the community and voluntary sector in many respects). At its best, the sector supports and encourages creativity: it analyses what works and what does not by trying new and flexible approaches. It explores new financing models, which deliver sustainability and value for money – examples include crowd funding; online fundraising; on-street direct-recruitment fundraising; social finance loan funding and the use of social impact bonds.

When at its best, the sector endeavours to involve users in the design and control of supports and services, and strives to empower communities to make their own decisions and shape their own futures. In this way, community and voluntary groups improve their communities, and in the process create wider societal value by adding additional resources to those available to the state (both financial and non-financial). This is social innovation in action!

In January 2016 The Wheel (with partner organisations Clann Credo and the Community Foundation for Ireland) published a research report *Let's Commission for Communities* which presented examples of social innovation in many of our members' work.

We found innovative practices where people living with personal challenges provide supports to others in similar situations. For example, at The Lakelands Area Retreat & Cancer Support Centre (LARCC) in County Westmeath, cancer patients have established a residential support centre for others in a similar situation – a process that has involved a highly creative and innovative use of local assets.

Similarly, we note innovation in the work of Keeping House in County Longford where local people have come together to provide housekeeping services for elderly people living in the community. It is a clear example of people working together to identify and respond to a local need, and it shows what people can achieve when they commit to creating a thriving community.

At Ability West in County Galway, we identified examples of service users living with intellectual disabilities being empowered. With their mantra of "nothing about me without me", service-users are encouraged to live the life of their choice with a whole raft of supports. The innovations range from an initiative with local colleges where students and service users are supported in friendships, to providing work experience opportunities for trainees by collaborating with local hairdressers and jewellery makers.

The Irish Men's Sheds movement is an excellent example of how social capital can underpin community cohesion. It follows a bottom up approach that places power in the hands of men to shape their own futures.

Pavee Point Traveller and Roma Centre's Health Project responded innovatively to research that indicated significant health inequalities between travellers and the settled community. They developed a primary healthcare programme to address information deficits and barriers to accessing healthcare for travellers - an example of the sector innovating to engage people from a specific community to support others within that community - and in the process provide training and employment opportunities.

All of these examples demonstrate social innovation in action by real communities for themselves and they are the tip of the iceberg of the hotbed of social innovation that constitutes Ireland's community and voluntary sector.

How can Government Further Foster and Support Social Innovation in the Sector?
Although additional funding is always welcome in the community and voluntary sector, government support for social innovation should not be limited to funding. The role of government certainly involves providing financing and removing impediments to social innovation, but for social

innovation to thrive, active supports and a supportive policy context are required.

Governments can support social innovators in a variety of ways. For example, they can facilitate networking between diverse individuals and organisations. Innovation or innovative thinking often happens because of interactions between people coming from different backgrounds and perspectives (e.g. the public, private and voluntary sectors). Government has the power to support and encourage this by establishing innovation hubs, where stakeholders can share best practice and explore new ideas to address challenges in areas like healthcare, social care and community development.

The European Commission supported the existing social innovation exchange network to host a Social Innovation Europe website (www.socialinnovationexchange.org). The aim of the website is to connect social innovators and bring people together to learn from one another.

In the US under the Obama administration, there was a White House Office of Social Innovation and Civic Participation, which hosted regular events to allow social innovators to come together. The sector can lead and play its part in the creation of such spaces, but it needs government support in the form of resources and access to networks.

Government can further support social innovation by encouraging community groups to own and manage local amenities, or by assisting social enterprises to develop the skills and knowledge needed to scale their solutions to a size that can win contracts to deliver services and attract further investment. Through such simple and practical supports, the community and voluntary sector can become an even stronger locus for social innovation.

However, in order to encourage and support this we need to ensure we have a policy environment that supports the sector to innovate into the future – and that means that we need to ensure that the community and voluntary sector is properly recognised, adequately resourced and sensitively regulated.

In this regard, The Wheel welcomes the statement in the Programme for a Partnership Government (Government of Ireland 2016:30) which states

We want to affirm the contribution of the community and voluntary sector to building a more just and prosperous society, and its strong focus on urban and rural regeneration. Community and voluntary organisations provide the human, social and community services in all key areas of our national life. In this work they contribute to the economy as well as create value for Irish society.

This recognition of the key role played by the community and voluntary sector in Ireland today is most welcome, and provides grounds for optimism that the state does indeed value the social innovation - and the societal value - that the sector delivers.

The Wheel is also very encouraged to see the programme for government committing to "increase funding levels to support the sector, and develop a multi-annual funding model that focuses on quality, effectiveness and efficiency" and to "produce a coherent policy framework and develop a strategy to support the community and voluntary sector and encourage a cooperative approach between public bodies and the community and voluntary sector" (Ibid).

Much work must still be done in this area to ensure that the necessary supports are delivered. We are also very conscious that the current political environment is particularly delicate and liable to change very quickly, so we must work to turn these commitments into reality as expediently as possible.

What Practical Steps can Government take to Support thriving Social Innovation in the Community and Voluntary Sector?

Basic preconditions for innovation include stability, an ability to plan and take calculated risks. Therefore, insecurely funded community and voluntary organisations must be placed on a firmer financial footing. While it is true that periods of challenge often leads to innovation, it is not good for service-providing organisations to be constantly fighting for their survival. One of the first things the government can do is to mainstream a multi-annual funding model which focuses on quality, effectiveness and efficiency.

If voluntary organisations are to innovate services then they must be able to plan and this in turn means there must be reasonable security of income. No one – neither profit- making company nor voluntary organisation - can plan for the future if they have no security of income.

Community and voluntary organisations raise funds from diverse sources, but many rely on a proportion of funding from the state. For those organisations that depend on statutory funding, many encounter difficulties in securing funds that allow for the full cost (including overheads for example) of the work that they do.

To address the security-of-income and the full-cost-recovery issues, we need a new framework for the statutory funding of voluntary organisations. This new framework should provide multi-annual funding that covers both the direct and indirect (or hidden) costs of running these organisations, and it should provide for the increased compliance costs that organisations now face in this era of increased regulation. We also need to improve the tax incentives system for donations to charities and voluntary organisations so that all donations are tax effective.

The public sector can also lead by example in fostering innovation in its own practices in the area of service design. There are many different approaches to fostering public-sector innovation. The Organisation for Economic Co-operation and Development (OECD) points out that approaches can range from developing whole-of-government innovation strategies that address the role of the public sector as innovator (e.g. Finland) to creating structures to support individual organisations in their innovation processes (e.g. Denmark) (OECD 2012:81)

In relation to 'partnerships with citizens and civil society' the OECD (2012:182) reports that the engagement of individual citizens and civil society organisations as partners in the delivery of public services (also known as co-production) can lead to higher user-satisfaction and reduced costs. The OECD also notes that partnerships that offer greater user control and ownership can transform the relationship between users and service professionals.

Here in Ireland, Genio brings Government and philanthropic funders together to help disadvantaged people live full lives in their communities. Genio - in collaboration with the Department of Health, the Health Service Executive and The Atlantic

Philanthropies - is currently helping to establish a Service Reform Fund[35] to support the implementation of reforms in disability and mental health services. Their approach has three elements:

- Innovation funding: where outcomes-focused and performance-managed funds are released on a competitive basis to encourage innovation and cost-effectiveness;
- Learning and skills: where key stakeholders are supported and trained to manage and implement required change; and
- Measuring impact: undertaking and commissioning research to measure impact.

The work of the OECD and Genio highlights a key point, namely that effectively funded and well-supported partnerships are important for social innovation to thrive. This is particularly true in Ireland because of the central role the sector plays in delivering social, health and community services. The insight is also particularly relevant to the Irish context because of the increasing use of outcomes-based commissioning approaches by state agencies (such as the HSE, Tusla and Pobal) to design and fund services.

It is relevant in this context to point to another important commitment in the Programme for Partnership Government, namely that government "will also ensure that all commissioning for human, social and community services takes place in a societal value framework" (Government of Ireland 2016:131).

The Wheel believes that if commissioning takes place within a societal value framework, then the sector has nothing to fear from this approach. Commissioning aimed at maximising societal value should deliver the best outcomes for communities in terms of the quality of services; provide the highest level of accountability to service users; ensure that services involve service users in the design process; and ensure that services are available to all who need them. This will maximise the societal value in the services and will ultimately have a positive impact.

---

[35] For more information see www.genio.ie/about-us/what-is-genio.

What Can the Sector do for Itself?

The Scottish Institute for Research and Innovation in Social Services (IRISS 2011) has researched and written about how we can create the right conditions for, and foster innovation within organisations. In summarising the findings of their literature review they found that 'culture, experience, skills, autonomy, leadership, favourable attitudes towards change and greater decentralisation and flexibility' are the main factors that help facilitate innovation (IRISS 2011). I will now briefly reflect on these factors in the Irish context;

I would argue that encouraging people to learn, take calculated risks and experiment is key. To do this the trustees and senior managers of community and voluntary organisations must set the tone and take calculated risks with public funds (something that they are not currently encouraged to do). We need to change the mind-set and encourage innovation by establishing cultures of innovation and calculated risk-taking (as opposed to cultures of routine and risk-aversion). Culture, however, is often the most difficult aspect of an organisation to define or even understand, let alone change. This will require changing public perceptions about the sector, changing the attitudes of boards to be open to calculated risk taking, and instilling confidence in managers to lead innovation by encouraging and expecting staff to generate new ideas as seen through changes in practice.

Secondly, our current workplace experience is key. We need to see the community and voluntary sector working more closely and collaboratively with private and public partners. As outlined above in the previous section innovation or innovative thinking often happens because of interactions between people from different backgrounds and perspectives (e.g. the public, private and voluntary sectors). Innovation hubs - where partners can share best practice and explore new ideas to address challenges in areas like healthcare, social care and community development offer opportunities for people to break out of their silos. IRISS (2011) states that "one feature of the most innovative organisations is that they are comfortable adopting ideas from diverse and sometimes surprising sources. To think successfully about new ideas, staff must have the ability to harvest ideas from a range of different sectors, places and individuals".

Skills are also key, and in times of rapid change like today, skills can rapidly become obsolete. This can be a big challenge for community and voluntary organisations where budgets for training and skills development have been cut disproportionately in recent years. IRISS (2011) also found organisations must have the authority and confidence to take measured risks. Funders need to understand and support calculated risk-taking by charities and non-profits. Chief executives should also view themselves as leaders rather than managers. Promoting favourable attitudes towards change is also important. IRISS (2011) suggests that appointing an 'innovation champion' (Howell *et al.* 2005) can encourage innovation in an organisation. Inflexible Service Level Agreements pose a challenge to innovation within the community and voluntary sectors, and indeed points to the requirement for proportions of service budgets agreed by public funders to include funding for supporting innovative practice.

Social Entrepreneurship
According to Social Entrepreneurs Ireland (SEI), Ireland is failing to address its social and environmental challenges fast enough. To do this, they say, we need new approaches and more innovative ideas. We need to challenge the status quo and look at these challenges from a different angle. The focus should be on effectiveness and impact. We need to fund results.

SEI is of the view that we are extremely fortunate in Ireland to have people across the country developing new solutions to our societal problems. Without support, however, they note that these ideas can struggle to make enough of an impact. With current challenges becoming more entrenched and new issues emerging, we know that we simply cannot afford to wait for these solutions to grow and scale on their own. We need to support SEI in their work to promote social entrepreneurs. Moreover, social innovators and social entrepreneurs should have access to the funding and support they need to scale and grow.

Similar initiatives, such as Change X and Social Innovation Fund Ireland, highlight innovative practice nationally and globally and demonstrate what is possible for communities. They provide tools for people and communities to take charge of their own problems and issues and create innovative responses to local challenges. We also need to acknowledge the great impact of social finance through the Social Finance Foundation and Clann Credo – and their willingness to take risks by funding innovations in community, voluntary and charitable organisations; risks many statutory funders may not be willing to take. More work needs to be done in the area of social impact bonds. We need more innovative thinking in how we can securely fund, and finance where appropriate, the work, and the calculated risks, of the work that the sector majors in, i.e. positive social change.

Learning Through Cooperation - The Need for North-South Ccollaboration
Ireland is a small island and in order to learn from and encourage each other we need to ensure that we have an open and accessible dialogue. We must encourage the enterprise and jobs departments as well as the social policy departments in both the North and the South to work together and to learn from each other – and this is more important than ever in the context of Brexit. We need to encourage civil society groups to develop their relationships and to work together to further their causes via learning from and understanding one and other.

Equally too, there is an important, and very positive role that networks and champions of social enterprise can play in this regard: the Irish Social Enterprise Network in Ireland and Social Enterprise Northern Ireland allow organisations which identify with the concept of social enterprise to network and connect with each other.

Conclusion
In recent years, we have witnessed a burgeoning of social innovation in the community, voluntary and charity sector. Policy makers are also beginning to support and promote social innovation and, in some cases, even act as social innovators themselves. Furthermore, we have witnessed an increase in government support for social investment through social impact bonds and other forms of loan finance. In turn, the community

and voluntary sector has successfully introduced the concept of societal value to the debate about the commissioning of public services. Moreover, we have witnessed the emergence of organisations like Social Entrepreneurs Ireland, Ashoka Ireland, Change X and Social Innovation Fund Ireland, as well as the social enterprise initiatives in many of the local development companies. The ecosystem is developing.

The proliferation of digital technologies has given the key actors, including governments and funders, new ways to engage with citizens and to connect diverse groups of people. This presents incredible opportunities to develop new solutions and fresh ideas.

Unfortunately, the participation in these initiatives still varies greatly. Governments and policy makers remain best positioned to establish and support the conditions socially innovative individuals and organisations need to flourish. We must also encourage the sharing of best practice so that policy makers from across the island of Ireland, from across Europe and from across the globe can learn from each other. Additionally, funders need to understand and support calculated risk-taking by charities and non-profits.

Some challenges will always be better addressed by investment in public services and infrastructure, however, the community, voluntary and charity sector will continue to play a big part in promoting social innovation in Ireland. Government, the community and voluntary sector, the public and funders can further augment the sector's role as an engine of social innovation if the actions outlined in this chapter are progressed. That way, we will continue to see a socially innovative community and voluntary sector thriving at the heart of a fair and just Ireland.

CHAPTER 7
SOCIAL INNOVATION IN COMMUNITY DEVELOPMENT

Philip McDermott and Lilian Seenoi-Barr

Introduction
The existence of the Irish border has posed numerous challenges in various fields of public administration and policy making since its establishment. However, the changing demographics of Ireland in the past two decades have raised new issues for those who have come to live on the island from elsewhere. Residency in areas close to an international frontier poses a number of further nuanced questions for migrants and also those community organisations working with such communities. This chapter specifically considers issues affecting international migrants and refugees who have come from beyond the UK and Ireland, with a primary focus on non-European citizens.

Drawing on the experiences of community groups representing ethnic minorities and migrants in Derry and Donegal this short chapter illustrates these difficulties. Both regions are also arguably peripheral in that they are somewhat detached from the core points of decision-making in Belfast and Dublin respectively which adds further dimensions to the challenges. In the Northern context immigration issues are not devolved and made in Westminster which adds a further detachment from these questions. The aims of this short chapter are to identify the key questions for migrant and refugee communities living in border locations and to consider interventions that may provide a first step in dissipating the major problems.

Context
The body of research on the experiences of migrants, refugees and ethnic minorities in Ireland, both north and south, has expanded immensely in the past two decades. One focus of the scholarship has been on the more integrative aspects such as language and cultural integration and the nature of living across two or more cultures (McDermott 2011; Feldman *et al.* 2008). Other literature has considered the impact of immigration on social policy (Migge and Gilmartin 2011). Connected to this has

been a widespread concern on race relations, social attitudes towards migrants, and questions around racism (See McDermott 2013; Lentin 2006; Fanning 2002; Hainsworth 1998; McKee 2016). There has, however, been a paucity of material which has covered how the Irish border impacts on these concerns. Indeed, when looking more specifically at the issues facing migrants and community organisations at border regions we begin to see the wider complexity posed by the border. The current insecurities arising from the UK's decision to leave the European Union (EU) potentially poses future challenges for European migrants living at the border. However, migrants and refugees from many non-European countries (especially form the Global South) have already been faced with a 'harder' border because of restrictions imposed by two separate immigration policies in Dublin and London. The current situation for these migrant groups sheds light on the complexities of the potential post-Brexit environment for all immigrants living in the region.

Donegal and Derry Context

In their respective jurisdictions, County Donegal and the Derry and Strabane District Council region have among the lowest populations of residents born outside the UK and Ireland. In 2016, for instance, the CSO noted that 6,000 people lived in Donegal who were born outside Ireland and the UK (around 3.5% of the population) (CSO 2016). By comparison, the Derry and Strabane District Council region in the most recent 2011 census was home to 7,641 of the same demographic (around 2.5% of the population) (NISRA 2011). To set these statistics in context the percentage of those in Ireland from outside the UK is 9%, while in Northern Ireland the figure was 4%.

The moderately small numbers of ethnic minorities and migrants, however, creates its own set of challenges as resources in areas that are already peripheral are much less developed than in other larger urban centres. For instance, public interpreters for specific languages may be difficult to source in urgent medical or legal cases. Also, schools may have a small number of children from non-English-speaking backgrounds and little in the way of funds or human resources to tackle such situations. Integration and resettlement for refugees in these locations also puts in context the challenges faced by these communities when living so close to the border which we return to later in this chapter. By comparison, in areas with larger numbers of migrants, interpreters may be available closer to the point of delivery, while schools with more linguistically diverse children may be able to pool resources such as classroom assistants. The border may be of less significance for refugees living in Dublin or Belfast than it does for those who live in Derry or Donegal.

We argue that the border certainly complicates the work of the community sector and the services provided for refugee and ethnic minorities are often duplicated when there is already strain on limited resources. Therefore, in peripheral areas like Derry and Donegal the potential for negative experiences of migrants is somewhat exacerbated. Given this challenging context the community and voluntary sector's support of migrant communities in these regions is critical in supporting migrants and refugee communities and to advise individuals of the limitations the border in the North-West imposes on them.

The North-West Migrants Forum was founded as a community initiative in February 2012 to provide support to refugees and asylum seekers in the Derry and Strabane region. The organisation champions the idea of intercultural dialogue as a social innovation tool to empower both the host and migrant populations. Given the proximity to the border the forum has been involved in collaborative work with community organisations in Donegal. This chapter draws on the experiences of both authors in their engagement with migrants from both sides of the border. These anecdotal interventions, we hope, provide a first step in illuminating some of the challenges faced by migrants in these areas. Whilst the examples utilised in this chapter are certainly not exhaustive they nonetheless provide important sentiments from grassroots which could begin to inform discussions at a wider policy level.

Key Issues and Challenges for Migrants at the Border
Perhaps the most prominent concern for many migrants at present is a political one, stemming from the UK's decision to leave the European Union after the June 2016 referendum. The resulting discussions have exposed the potential difficulties which might arise for EU migrants living in Ireland if the

current 'border dynamic' is to change. However, the existence of the border has always been a very real issue for those coming from outside the EU – especially from countries in the Global South. From our observations such groups have already faced a 'hard border' which already impedes their 'freedom of movement' in what others regard as an integrated socio-economic region. Nancy Wonders (2006:64) notes that globalisation has created somewhat of a myth regarding the permeability of borders and that instead most borders are merely semi-permeable and are deliberately "constructed to facilitate the entry of some but to deter the entry of others". The Irish Border is no exception. The potential changes in the coming years may extend such semi-permeability to a larger number of migrants from European countries and thus exacerbate issues such as public service access, daily life and indeed community development work itself. Therefore, it is perhaps an opportune moment to reflect on how the border already poses challenges (for many non-EU migrants) in these areas.

Accessing Services

Cross-border mechanisms developed through the peace process have certainly improved opportunities for most of those living in the north and south to share resources such as healthcare. However, such privileges have not always been extended to most migrant communities beyond the EU. For example, refugees with humanitarian protection or full refugee status in Northern Ireland cannot access healthcare in Ireland even when service provision is geographically closer. Likewise, we also see examples of the same practices where those in Ireland have not been able to access resources in Northern Ireland. We are aware of a number of cases where lives, including those of children, have been put at risk. In one case a child who could have received treatment in Dublin was forced instead to wait on available treatment in London. In these cases, immigration restrictions have stopped movement across the border, even in cases of extreme emergency. Bureaucracy ultimately impacts on 'human' decisions and the wellbeing of the communities in question.

There are also issues with regard to education, where there is restricted access to further and higher-level study. For example, for those from non-EU backgrounds wishing to enter higher education this has been rendered extremely complex and costly. It is almost impossible as fees for such communities are regularly set at the same level for other international students coming from the Global North. This, coupled with a limited number of schemes to assist higher education for migrants and refugees from the Global South is not conducive to attracting vulnerable populations or tackling social marginalisation. By contrast 'local students' from Donegal and Derry can freely travel between jurisdictions for education and access lower, but not insignificant, fees. The result is that there is much more cross-border traffic of students from white European backgrounds whilst the intellectual capital of refugees is not utilised effectively as a resource.

As noted above the smaller numbers of ethnic minorities often results in less developed services in border areas. Often, because of visa restrictions, human resources and expertise from within particular communities cannot be shared. This has been clearly illustrated in the field of public interpreting where examples have arisen whereby migrants who are themselves qualified interpreters in Donegal cannot travel to Derry to assist emergencies because of their own visa restrictions. In such circumstances, alternative arrangements from elsewhere in Northern Ireland are required which adds significantly to the cost of the service due to additional mileage and hours required. Sourcing of these resources is already major challenge in Ireland so it is incumbent that innovative ways are found to alleviate these concerns (McDermott 2011: 119).

Of course, these are only a number of small examples but indicate how the lack of resource sharing and information sharing, coupled with the complex visa and immigration system, is impacting on the effectiveness of public service delivery in regions with already limited resources.

Daily Life of Migrants

A further concern which we frequently encounter is that there are a number of issues relating to general daily life which are impacted by the border. Some of these may initially appear trivial but they have a significant impact on the settlement, wellbeing and quality of life of individuals and communities.

Consequently, isolation and alienation is a reality for many small communities living on other sides of the border as they cannot engage and support each other due to the restrictions on their movement across a border which for so many others appears 'fluid' and 'frictionless'.

For example, we are aware of many families from Africa and Asia living in Derry who have been unable to avail of extended support networks in neighbouring Donegal and vice-versa. One of the most frequent comments relates to the inability of communities to travel to the other jurisdiction in order to acquire foods which relate to their spiritual or cultural needs – a critical issue for many diaspora communities (Mintz 2008). For example, some individuals from African communities in Derry cannot cross to Letterkenny where there is a wider selection of foods from Africa on sale. In such cases some individuals take a much longer round trip to Belfast or other towns such as Dungannon. However, many, knowingly or unknowingly, cross the border with the risks that this entails. Likewise, those living in Donegal are faced with the same predicaments and all of the restrictions that this places on their daily lives. Nevertheless, breaching immigration rules in this way can jeopardise the path to citizenship and risk detention. Individuals and families have been penalised for crossing the border, even solely for the purposes of leisure – like a trip to the seaside. Such examples of large risk along 'porous' borders, for what might be viewed as fairly trivial reasons, have been very common among many other diaspora communities in other comparable contexts internationally (Núñez and Heyman 2007).

In some cases, the complexities around visas, residency and crossing the border adversely impact on family life. One case which exemplifies this intricacy involved a woman from East Africa who married a Derry man. She had originally arrived in Ireland under an Irish visa for an initial period of two years. Whilst her husband lived in a house in Derry she was forced to stay with relatives in County Donegal. It was only when she applied for a British visa and this application was being processed that she was allowed to live with her husband in Derry in their marital home. At this time this individual was expecting her second child but when she went into labour she could not access healthcare in Derry's Altnagelvin hospital. This was because her permit had not been approved and she was instead forced to acquire paid medical care in Ireland. This is only one example of a plethora of cases where eventual 'permission' to cross the border does not necessarily lead to full 'inclusion'.

Another concern that we have noted in our work is the increasing level of racial profiling in areas close to the border by both policing authorities. A number of families with permanent residency have commented on how they have been frequently stopped by authorities when they are in a car with registration plates from the other jurisdiction. In these cases, they have been stopped and questioned about their citizenship and legal status. The individuals who have experienced such incidents have considered and interpreted that these are examples of clear racial profiling. Indeed this practice, it has been noted, has deterred even those migrants with full residency status from crossing the border.

Challenges for the Community Sector

All of the issues described above have also had an impact in restricting the means through which communities can be supported across borders. Firstly, there are variances in legislation and integration strategies which drive community organisations in diverse directions with different expectations from funders. The community development sector in the north has frequently focused on the peace process and the divisions between protestant and catholic communities. Some critics have argued that this process renders ethnic minority and migrant communities as somewhat marginal. Indeed, the resources and funding for cross border work under peace and regeneration projects also follows this pattern (See Byrne *et al.* 2009). Therefore, there is more scope for integrated funding streams across the border to help migrants in border regions with the problems raised in the previous two sections.

As noted in the previous section, the visa restrictions which affect certain communities also have a knock-on impact on the community sector itself. For example, there are a number of community workers who themselves are in the position where their residency status stops them from travelling to the neighbouring jurisdiction. Unfortunately, this means that certain expertise and knowledge cannot be used for the benefit of the entire border region. This has been especially pertinent in sharing information about different policy procedures in relation to immigration. Also, this has had more practical implications such as in the field of interpreting where community organisations with expertise in particular languages cannot assist one another on a cross-border basis.

More generally, a clear issue for the community development sector is that, despite the clear implications for such groups, migrant voices from the grassroots are missing on the policy debates on cross border issues. This has become all the more important in the current climate where a border which is already 'hard' for some communities may become even more of an issue for a greater range of migrant communities. The ethnic minority and refugee community development sector itself must push for a more integrated approach to ensure that voice from the grassroots level is heard in these extremely important questions.

Conclusions and Recommendations for Future Discussion
This short chapter merely identifies a few of the key issues in relation to the experiences of migrants and ethnic minorities at border regions. However, the reflection on our experiences and our discussions with communities and organisations indicate clear patterns. Therefore, to conclude we lay out a number of points which could provide future avenues of discussion.

A border region strategy for ethnic minorities and refugees would be a useful step forward in consolidating and improving practices towards integration and diversity. At a political level, cross border agencies and the North South Ministerial Council, which provide the opportunity for political dialogue on issues of mutual concern, could take a bolder role in generating discussion on immigration and diversity in their future meetings. This is a highly appropriate point at which to initiate these conversations given the changing dynamics associated with 'Brexit'.

Decision-making processes are complex. However, assumptions are often used by practitioners when dealing with migrants. Community organisations could engage more with public agencies such as the police, immigration officials and the criminal justice system and schools in both the north and south.

We note that there are many innovative voluntary initiatives which have the potential to make public services, such as these, more effective. This could be achieved simply through better opportunities for the dissemination of knowledge acquired at grassroots level on both sides of the border to public agencies. There is however, to date, no specific mechanism to connect community organisations effectively to service providers on a cross-border basis.

More knowledge is required on the experiences of migrants living in border regions. For this reason, qualitative research on the perspectives of migrants is an important means to capture the more human elements of these complex experiences. Often, we see exclusive discussions which rely largely on statistics whereas more interpretivist research would capture the range of feeling and understanding by individuals and communities themselves.

SECTION III
SECTORS

CHAPTER 8
'A NEW WAY FORWARD' – THE DEVELOPMENT OF A SOCIAL ENTERPRISE STRATEGY FOR THE IRISH CRIMINAL JUSTICE SECTOR[36]

Siobhán Cafferty

Introduction

In recent years, the number of social enterprises (SEs) operating within criminal justice jurisdictions across Europe has grown considerably as they are increasingly seen as an innovative model of overcoming barriers to employment for people with criminal convictions. Combining a business model with a social mission, SEs are particularly attractive to those working with offenders, as securing employment plays a key role in recidivism rates. Income generating businesses, based in both prison and community settings, are creating employment options for those most distant from the labour market as a result of their previous criminal convictions and lifestyles. This, in turn, lends itself towards reduced re-offending rates, creating safer communities and fewer victims.

Despite the proven successes of SEs in criminal justice sectors across Europe, it remained uncharted territory here in Ireland until May 2017 when the Department of Justice and Equality made a decision to support innovation by launching their Social Enterprise Strategy (SE Strategy). Based on primary research conducted with key stakeholders from the Department, the Irish Prison Service, the Probation Service and the community and voluntary sector, this chapter briefly outlines the process of developing this strategy, considered a cutting edge approach to addressing long term exclusion from the labour market for people with convictions. It charts the journey from primary research to the publication of the innovative and forward thinking SE strategy co-owned by the Department of Justice and

---

[36] This chapter is based on an adapted and updated version of an article published in the *Irish Probation Journal*, volume 13, 2016: Cafferty, S., McCarthy, O. & Power, C.,"Risk and Reward: The development of Social Enterprise within the Criminal Justice Sector in Ireland – Some policy implications". This chapter is produced with permission of the editors of the *Irish Probation Journal*.

Equality and its executive agencies, the Irish Prison Service and the Probation Service.

Context

In the past 20 years, the nature, type and frequency of crimes committed in Ireland has changed significantly with more serious offences being committed than ever before. A direct result of this was a 100% increase in the prison population between the years 1997 and 2011. Rising levels of drug related crime, violent offences, prolific offenders and gangland activity have challenged the criminal justice system to respond effectively, as well as, increasing the financial burden on the State. According to the Irish Penal Reform Trust (2017), there were 3,674 people in prison on December 20th 2016. With the average cost of an 'available, staffed prison space' in 2015 being €68,628 (this figure can rise to €97,000 in some high risk prisons), the total cost for imprisoning people each year is significant. It is in the interest of all citizens that these figures are tackled effectively, and with a long term vision, so the number of victims of crime reduces as the number of people committing offences falls.

The research upon which the Department of Justice and Equality's SE strategy, and this chapter, is based examined the potential role of social enterprise (SE) in reducing re-offending rates. It is widely known that the securing of employment plays a significant role in desisting from crime (Farrington *et al.* 1996; Maruna 1997; Visher *et al.* 2005; Social Exclusion Unit 2002) and as such is enshrined in legislation as a key target for criminal justice agencies when working with their clients (The Probation Act 1907). Research also indicates however that the motivation to remain crime free post release reduces over an extended period of time in the absence of on-going supports to the offender (Tripodi *et al.* 2010; Visher *et al.* 2005). SE as an approach to providing supported employment for offenders has been under-utilised within the sector.

Significant amounts of research have shown that the rate of unemployment is disproportionately higher amongst prison populations (Social Exclusion Unit 2002; Farrington *et al.* 1996; IPRT 2014). Similarly, a study conducted by Mair and May (1997) identified that of 3,299 offenders on probation in the UK, only 21% were employed (Cosgrove *et al.* 2011). This figure mirrors the statistics for Ireland; over 70% of prisoners state that they are unemployed on committal and a similar percentage self-report as not having any particular trade or occupation (IPRT 2017).

The Theory of Desistance (Maruna 1997) argues that being in gainful employment is a key factor in reducing or desisting from crime. Desistance from crime is defined as, "the long-term abstinence from criminal behaviour among those for whom offending had become a pattern of behaviour" (McNeill *et al.* 2012:3). While employment is recognised in legislation, policies and evidence-based practice as being significantly important, a criminal record is a significant impediment to securing employment. Social enterprises not only provide employment opportunities and training for people with criminal convictions; they do so in a supportive, client centred environment where other factors leading to offending behaviour can also be addressed (Nicholson 2010:17).

Interest in social enterprise has increased significantly in recent years due to an awareness of its potential to address deep-rooted societal issues while operating from a model of inclusion and community development. In the UK, specific social enterprises have targeted people with a history of offending in an attempt to reduce recidivism[37]. This growing interest has also been influenced by the global financial downturn; austerity measures implemented in many First World countries mean that communities cannot rely on the state to provide resources or services.

Social Enterprise Defined

SE presents a different and refreshing way of doing things that recognises societal issues and need as well as being inclusive of those most affected by disadvantage and/or the financial crisis. However, defining what a SE actually is can prove difficult as there is no universally accepted definition (Gardner *et al.* 2014; Forfas 2013; Eustace and Clark 2009; Everett 2009). Having analysed a number of European definitions, the Forfas Report

---

[37] Café Britannia on the grounds of HMP Norwich prison is one example: https://www.cafebritannia.co.uk .

(2013:2) proposes the following definition of SEs in an Irish context:

> A social enterprise is an enterprise: i) that trades for a social/societal purpose; ii) where at least part of its income is earned from its trading activity; iii) is separate from government; and iv) where the surplus is primarily re-invested in the social objective.

While awaiting the forthcoming National Social Enterprise Strategy[38] and its agreed definition, the Department of Justice and Equality, through its SE Steering Committee, elected to adopt this Forfas definition as a working description for the purposes of their strategy.

Common to all definitions is the social focus or mission, income generating capacity and reinvestment of profits back into the organisation in order to benefit the community and wider society (Gardner *et al.* 2014). Despite these numerous definitions, there still remains a lack of clarity on certain elements such as the amount of surplus to be re-invested, legal structures and the level of independence. In addition, SEs are part of the 'third sector'. The 'third sector' is the umbrella term given to any organisation that is independent from a state but may receive state-funded support and may contribute to the delivery of public services (Eustace and Clark 2009).

Research Findings – The Foundations of a Strategy

The primary research[39] upon which the Social Enterprise Strategy is based explored the risks and rewards of social enterprise within the Irish criminal justice sector and was completed as part of the requirements of an MBS in Co-operative and Social Enterprise with University College Cork. In addition to the academic focus, the research was intended to assist the Department of Justice, and its executive agencies, to explore possibilities for the development of the social enterprise sector in Ireland.

---

[38] The Department of Arts, Heritage, Regional, Rural & Gaeltacht Affairs have the responsibility of developing the National Social Enterprise Strategy which is expected to be published by the end of 2017 or early 2018.
[39] Cafferty *et al.* 2016.

Semi-structured interviews with eight key stakeholders were undertaken to seek an understanding of their perceptions in relation to the role of social enterprise in the criminal justice system and the risks and rewards of developing social enterprise in a criminal justice and integration setting.

Four stakeholder groups were identified as having views or positions relevant to the research. These were relevant senior decision making staff within the Department of Justice, Probation Service and Irish Prison Service as well as a representative from a community based organisation working with criminal justice clients and with experience of operating a social enterprise. The focus was on groups whose remit included rehabilitation and/or the ability to contribute to policy development in the area.

Key stakeholders were purposively sampled due to their influence in relation to policy within the criminal justice or social enterprise support sectors.

This research found that there were a number of policy implications and other structural barriers that needed to be overcome in order to support the development of social enterprises within the criminal justice field. Following a thematic analysis of the findings, 14 themes emerged. These themes have been synopsised here[40]:

1. Recognition by decision makers that there are limitations in knowledge and awareness of SE within Ireland.

Seven of the eight respondents reported that their level of awareness and understanding of what SE is and how SE is defined was very limited. Of this group, none had practical or first-hand experience of SE. One stakeholder had practical experience of having developed a SE for people with criminal convictions. Respondents stated that they were unsure of how to define a SE as being distinct from a charity or other small business and provided examples within their dialogue of this lack of clarity. As a result of a lack of clarity on the exact definition of a SE, respondents were unsure if particular businesses they were familiar with were operating as SEs. When asked about whether SE was a genuinely new model or simply a

---

[40] Full version of the 14 themes can be found in Cafferty et al. 2016.

reworking of previously trialled models, there was a clear agreement (7 of 8 respondents) that SE presented a tangibly different way of providing services, if done well. The main reason for the difference was perceived to be the core business model, and the reality that this brought to the training aspects of the programme. Despite an acknowledged limited awareness of SE, respondents felt that the model had relevance for the future criminal justice system. SEs were regarded as offering alternative ways of doing business that benefit individuals, families and communities.

2. Acknowledgement of the potential benefits of SE in the criminal justice sector.

All eight respondents reported that they would like to see the development of SEs within the criminal justice system increase as they believe SE offers significant potential for the welfare of the client group and their families, and for the state and its agencies in relation to efficiency and service outcomes. Benefits articulated could be divided into two groups: benefits to the criminal justice system and benefits to the offender or individual.

3. SEs need to be responsive to individual client and customer need, which requires flexibility in funding structures.

Responsiveness and ability to quickly adapt to the demands and needs of various stakeholders was also an emerging theme. The need for responsiveness poses a challenge in relation to the standard funding structures of traditional grant aid funding where services are expected to have detailed plans and key performance indicators, and to meet these with minimal changes over the funding period. These funding requirements may constrain or not be appropriate to the environment that new start-up businesses operate within[41]. However, the ability of SE to take a more responsive approach to client needs was also viewed as a positive. These points highlight the need for any

---

[41] Steve Blank (2012) the well-known writer on enterprise, states that, "Most start-ups are facing a series of unknowns – unknown customer segments, unknown customer needs, unknown product feature set, etc. Writing a static business *plan* first adds no value to *starting* a company, as the plan does not represent the iterative nature of the *search* for the model".

funding structures to take account of the fact that a successful start-up will generally require significant flexibility in how it runs its business and that this responsiveness is required in order for the needs of the business and client to be met.

4. The need for leadership and for specific entrepreneurial skills.
Respondents highlighted that existing structures within the state or currently funded community based organisations (CBOs) are not likely to have, or do not have, the expertise to initiate or develop organisations on a business (income generating, profit and loss model) rather than grant funded model. Leadership was seen as being needed at two levels: firstly, to establish SE within the criminal justice sector, and secondly, to establish and run new SEs. The view was that without dedicated and experienced leadership, change was unlikely to happen in any significant manner. It was noted that, at the current time, adequate expertise was unlikely to reside in either state organisations or on the board of traditional grant funded CBOs. However, in both cases CBOs and state agencies respondents saw the solution as being either the co-opting of sufficient additional expertise, or in the case of CBOs, funding new organisations which had been explicitly established with appropriate levels of internal competence and experience to develop and manage a SE.

5. The need for organisations to maintain the focus on personal development and avoid mission drift.
The primary goal of SEs operating in this sector is the personal development of clients, the enhancement of life skills and employment-focused skills. However, a business focus is also important to ensure the viability of the SE. It was noted that, at times, there was a challenge in maintaining this dual focus.

6. A range of risks exist that are particular to SE: liability and decision making.
There were two main risk areas identified by respondents that affected SE in a way which was not experienced in relation to other grant funded services. These were firstly concerns around financial and governance liabilities, and whether this would fall to state agencies, and secondly risks related to closing down

unsuccessful SEs; how this decision would be made and the impact of it. The fear of financial failure and risks associated with it were mentioned by a number of respondents.

The potential financial risks and future liabilities of SEs were noted as factors which have hindered their development up to this point. However, respondents noted that with adequate structures and agreements in place from establishment, through the independent legal structures of the SE, these risks and liabilities can be reduced and managed.

7. Public relations – risk and reward in relation to the development of SE.

There were mixed views on whether SE could have a more potentially positive or negative impact on public opinion. However, respondents were clear that the introduction of SE would require careful consideration and management of PR, in order to either avoid potentially damaging media coverage or to optimise the potential benefits of this development. However, there is likely to be more of a spotlight on SEs than other new businesses. The contextualisation of managing failure would need to be considered from the outset. Respondents noted a range of both potentially positive and negative views regarding the public relations of a SE employing people with a background in offending. An awareness of and sensitivity to customers' needs and concerns as well as the potential negative public perception of state funded SEs competing with non-subsidised private companies, needs to be addressed in the marketing plan for any SE of this nature.

8. Attitudes to commercialism and the need for a wider culture change are barriers to SE development.

Five respondents referenced the fact that Ireland had a different governmental culture to other countries that had invested significantly in SE and that these factors would need to change in order for SE to become supported at the mainstream state agency level. Some of the cultural majority understandings or views that respondents highlighted as potential barriers that may need to be addressed included a fear of business or a general understanding that 'money and profit is not our concern'.

9. The need for clear interagency and interdisciplinary structures to support decision making in relation to SE.

Respondents stated that in order for SE to be developed within the Irish criminal justice sector, there is a need to establish a cross agency structure to support and fund new SEs. This steering group structure was seen as essential to the engagement of individual state agencies and as a response to concerns around the risks related to SE and potential failure of individual enterprises. There was agreement that key partners would include, ideally the Probation Service, the Irish Prison Service, and the Department of Justice, as well as individuals from the business and SE community with expertise in areas such as finance and procurement.

10. The need for funders to understand SE value propositions[42].

The need for senior staff within state agencies to have a better understanding of SE has already been noted. Aligned to this is the need for an agreement on the value proposition of SE that takes into account internal standards and research. The notion of the need for a return on investment was well understood, however little other detail or concrete definitions were offered in relation to value and the outcomes that could be expected.

11. The need for SE to be contextualised within the overall criminal justice service provision continuum of care.

The need for SE to have a defined place within the criminal justice service was noted. Respondents stated that there is a clear need for new SE ventures to be able to articulate precisely why this pathway was appropriate and useful to them, and what separated it from other options. SE could potentially provide supports to bridge the gap from courses or supported training programmes to employment. This gap is significant in some existing training programmes.

---

[42] A brief business or marketing statement that clearly describes the benefits to a customer as to why they should buy a particular product or service. (Emerson 2003).

12. The role of state agencies as customers.

Another emerging theme was that the state has a role to play not just in supporting development and innovation of SE but also in purchasing or hiring from SE projects.

13. Need for statutory leadership to support change in relation to procurement.

The issue of awarding of contracts to SE through open tender processes was discussed with interviewees. It was noted by the majority that value for money was a major consideration of all procurement processes. Respondents were also asked about whether they supported the idea of procurement processes giving weighting for social value, i.e. employment of ex-prisoners[43]. This highlights potential for additional training and information in relation to the way that the state and SE operate in relation to procurement within other jurisdictions. Five respondents supported this idea.

In relation to large service contracts (i.e. cleaning, maintenance, laundry etc.) it was noted that there may be legal issues in relation to changes in contracting arrangements, that may present barriers to the state contracting SEs. While it was acknowledged that there would be both practical and perception related challenges that would require specific targeted responses, the need for the criminal justice sector to explore their role as customer alongside that of funder was highlighted as requiring further consideration.

14. The challenge for new social enterprises in developing trust with customers.

The need for new social enterprises to gain the trust of potential customers – and the challenge this presents – was seen as a key issue by the majority of respondents. This was noted especially in reference to services where ex offenders may have access to people's goods, space or private information. Trust was viewed as being intimately connected with governance and it was recognised that senior staff within a social enterprise had a core

---

[43] 'Social or community benefit clauses' (CBCs) provide a means of achieving sustainability in public contracts by allowing a procurement officers to build in a range of economic, environmental or social conditions into the delivery of contracts (Social enterprise and Entrepreneurship Taskforce 2012)

role to play in relation to developing trust with potential commercial customers and establishing trust in the services quality, a component of which would be related to security and safety. There is significant potential for criminal justice services to become customers of emerging SEs that can provide a useful service. However, issues in relation to trust and service quality will need to be managed and a core component of this will be down to the leadership of new SEs. External quality marks could also be a useful aid in developing customer interest and trust.

Journey to a New Way Forward

Following the completion of the primary research outlined above, a number of key actions were taken to support the development of social enterprise as an alternative approach to creating employment opportunities for people with criminal convictions.

As a first step, a number of key stakeholders were invited to an initial discussion workshop, hosted by the Probation Service, in February 2016. The purpose of this workshop was to get representatives from the statutory, public and private sectors, researchers and academics as well as social enterprise support organisations[44] to see how we could collectively address the structural and policy barriers identified by the research.

Following this initial discussion workshop, it was agreed that a steering committee should be established to oversee the development of a social enterprise strategy for the sector as well as driving social enterprise initiatives as a way of increasing employment rates for people with criminal convictions. The establishment of the SE Steering Committee represented an alternative and complementary approach to existing employment models in the sector as well as demonstrating a commitment to innovation from the Department of Justice and Equality.

---

[44] Attendees at this initial discussion workshop represented the following agencies: Department of Justice and Equality, Probation Service, Irish Prison Service, Department of Social Protection, Irish Social Enterprise Networks, Social Finance Foundation, Social Enterprise Task Force, entrepreneurs, academics, researchers and representatives from the community and voluntary sector.

The first meeting of the newly established SE Steering Committee[45] took place in May 2016 where the future direction of the committee was discussed and agreed. Terms of reference were developed with the action of recruiting a SE Project Manager to drive the development of the strategy as a priority. The committee meets on a quarterly basis.

A SE Project Manager, with experience of working with in the criminal justice sector, was identified, appointed and commenced work in the role at the end of November 2016. This appointment was approved by the Department of Justice and Equality and is jointly supported by the Irish Prison Service and Probation Service with the Project Manager reporting directly to the SE Steering Committee. The manager is accommodated by the Probation Service and supported by a Principal Officer in the Irish Prison Service.

In consultation with the SE Steering Committee, and drawing on the research findings, the Project Manager develop a 12-month action plan in order to support the development of a SE Strategy as well as other key activities for the sector. This action plan focuses on five key objectives with seven practical actions and formed the foundation for the new SE strategy.

A New Way Forward – Social Enterprise Strategy 2017 -2019
The Department of Justice and Equality SE Strategy was officially launched by Tánaiste and Minister for Justice, Ms. Frances Fitzgerald TD on May 15th 2017 in Mountjoy Prison. The strategy covers a three year operational period from 2017 to 2019 with a commitment to conduct a mid-term review to ensure greater alignment with the National SE Strategy once published.

The Department of Justice and Equality are the first government department to officially launch their strategy supporting the development of social enterprises while awaiting the publication of the national strategy. This is a most unusual approach as in other European countries development of the

---

[45] Committee members include: Vivian Geiran, Michael Donnellan, Domini Kemp(entrepreneur, chef & author), Kieran Moylan(Principal Officer, Care & Rehabilitation Directorate, Irish Prison Service), Brendan Whelan(CEO, Social Finance Foundation), Noel Dowling(Principal, Prisons & Probation Unit, Dept of Justice & Equality), John Gallagher(Social Enterprise Task Force) and Siobhán Cafferty(SE Project Manager).

third sector is triggered by the publication of a national strategy which then filters down to the various government departments to adopt and implement. In launching their social enterprise strategy ahead of the long awaited national approach, the Department of Justice and Equality are leading the way and showing their commitment to try different methods of increasing employment for people with criminal convictions. This ice breaking approach brings with it many challenges as national policies and infrastructure is being examined through a different lens for the first time. In some cases, current policies need to be amended or developed in order to support social enterprises in a way that existing grant funded models do not require. While essential, these changes would be made easier if a national social enterprise policy was already in place and being implemented.

The Department of Justice and Equality strategy centres around a four pillar structure and is underpinned by a vision, mission and principles for implementation. The figure below outlines the four pillar structure.

Figure 8.1 – The four pillars of 'A new way forward – Social Enterprise Strategy 2017 -2019'[46]

The strategy is co-owned by the Department of Justice and Equality and its executive agencies, the Irish Prison Service and

---

[46] Reproduced with permission from the Department of Justice & Equality.

the Probation Service. It is designed to operate within and support a wider employment focused approach by both agencies than is currently in existence. It is not designed to replace current approaches along the continuum of care but rather complement them by providing another option for progression. The SE strategy was also developed with full recognition that the very nature of commercial businesses is that a certain percentage will not succeed. By its very nature, the SE strategy is based upon an acknowledgement that progress will be maximised by adopting a partnership, inter-agency, multi-departmental approach.

The four pillar structure is supported by specific objectives with key performance indicators for each. A total of 24 objectives are named, all designed to create the right conditions for SE initiatives within the criminal justice sector.

Pillar One – Creating Enabling Environments for SE

This pillar focuses on addressing specific structural barriers to developing SE within the sector and as such, is underpinned by the largest number of objectives, 10 in total. In brief, these include:

- Address insurance restrictions for businesses, including social enterprises, who are open to recruit people with convictions.

- Prisoner pay for engagement in external employment including social enterprises.

- Establish a gaps and blocks reporting process that facilitates the capturing of any unforeseen barriers to the development of SEs within the sector and subsequent solutions.

- Explore the feasibility and implementation of Certificates of Employability in Ireland to increase employment opportunities and to address licensing issues for SEs and for employers in general.

- Ensuring progression from SEs into the mainstream workplace.

- Explore the introduction of a ring fenced seed funding stream specifically to support SE actions with in the sector and one that facilitates access to existing SE supports.

- Structures and supports are developed and implemented to facilitate the assessment of SE applications to the Irish Prison Service and Probation Service.
- Ensure procurement processes are accessible to SEs through the implementation of social clauses and social enterprise preferred clauses in accordance with the Office of Government Procurement guidelines (forthcoming).
- Liaise with the Irish Association for the Social Integration of Offender (IASIO) in order to link people with convictions into SEs, as well as other referral routes as an alternative progression pathway.
- Develop a positive media strategy highlighting the multi-faceted benefits of social enterprise activities within the criminal justice sector.

Pillar Two: Developing Leadership & Capacity
The four objectives of pillar two aim to increase awareness of the role and function of SEs as well as increasing specific skills and expertise in the area of developing social enterprises. They include:
- Develop a range of training supports and resources on SE for people working within statutory management roles, procurement, community based organisations(CBOs) and prison environments.
- Accessing resource to support the implementation of the strategy.
- In collaboration with social enterprises, as well as community organisations with relevant expertise, organise awareness raising events on all aspects of SE targeting criminal justice personnel and agencies.
- Develop learning communities to support knowledge sharing in new and existing SEs.

<u>Pillar Three: Increasing access to markets & developing SE business partnerships</u>

Finding the most appropriate and effective routes to market places will be crucial for the success and sustainability of SEs operating within this sector. Similarly, ensuring a person's journey through the criminal justice system maximises their chance of securing employment on release is also essential. Pillar Three addresses these directly under seven objectives:

- Maximise links between prison and CBO-based training to ensure it is labour market led and meets the needs of employers, including social enterprises.
- Liaise with specific employer organisations, including social businesses, in conjunction with IASIO, to conduct an employer needs assessment for labour market areas with employment gaps.
- Explore the feasibility and promotion of new and existing incentivised employment schemes for businesses open to recruiting people with convictions, in conjunction with IASIO.
- Support prison and community based work place training schemes to sell products.
- Develop a universal brand and marketing plan for bringing goods and services made within criminal justice agencies to the marketplace.
- Explore promotion and sale of products on a purely commercial basis with retail partners, to enable stand-alone testing and marketability of products produced. Seek a relevant main street partner for selected product(s), which would be marketed on a commercial basis as well as through a designated pilot outlet.
- Pilot the effectiveness of an urban outlet market facility in assisting with the commercial sale of goods produced within criminal justice agencies.

<u>Pillar Four: Measuring Impact</u>

The final pillar of the strategy is designed to measure the impact of this new approach and specifically answer the question, how do we know its working? To this end, pillar four contains three objectives to ensure the impact of SEs can be measured through a number of lenses; personal progress for the person with the convictions, their families and community benefits as well as fewer victims and a reduced burden on the exchequer. The three objectives of pillar four are:

- Establish an input and outcomes framework for the measurement of all new schemes and SEs with guidance and measurement tools to include measurement of commercial activity as well as social impact.
- Develop national information gathering system to support analysis of impact of national programmes.
- Undertake cost benefit analysis/Social Return on Investment (SROI) on any significant new programmes to measure social value impact across a number of variables.

Conclusion

People with education and training, who are in employment, are less likely to offend. This is the principal theme underpinning the Social Enterprise Strategy 2017 -2019 launched by the Department of Justice and Equality and co-owned by its executive agencies. As such, it is the responsibility of these agencies to lead the way in ensuring they are supporting existing employment initiatives, as well as seeking out new and innovative approaches to maximise employment opportunities for people with convictions.

It was in recognition of the positive impact that securing employment plays on reducing re-offending rates and the natural fit with the objectives of social enterprise activity, that the Department of Justice and Equality sought, pursued and are leading the way with their SE strategy.

The four pillar structure of this strategy highlights that in order for social enterprises to flourish and reach their true potential within the criminal justice sector, structural and policy changes need to be implemented. In many cases, change can only take place when a number of supporting factors align simultaneously. In this case, the Department of Justice and Equality strategy only came about because the right key stakeholders were in decision making positions at the same time. They all shared the desire to do things differently, to create more opportunities for people coming through the system while at the same time, creating safer communities. Essentially, they shared the same vision for social enterprise. The development of a specific strategy supporting social enterprise is a significant step forward however, a robust implementation plan to ensure all 24 objectives are completed is now the main focus and direction for the Department of Justice and Equality, the Irish Prison Service, the Probation Service and in particular, the SE Steering Committee. With the SE strategy providing a strong foundation upon which the sector can develop, it is strongly anticipated that within a 12 month period, numerous case studies of successful social enterprises employing people with convictions will be a reality.

CHAPTER 9
SOCIAL INNOVATION IN THE HEALTH SECTOR; A CASE STUDY OF IRELAND

Rodd Bond and Lucia Carragher

Introduction

Social innovations can be seen to refer to new ideas (products, services and models) that meet social needs and create new social relationships or collaborations. That is to say, they are innovations that are both good for society and enhance society's capacity to act (Murray Caulier-Grice and Mulgan 2010). Interest in social innovations has grown over recent years amongst policy makers, academics, and wider society in general because of the potential to solve big social challenges. This includes contemporary challenges around economic crises, widening inequalities, ageing populations, increasing levels of chronic disease, migration and urbanization, and environmental damage and climate change. Challenges which, as Murray *et al.* (2010) point out, market solutions and the classic tools of government policy have failed to address; the market by itself has no incentive or appropriate model to use to solve many of these issues and governments' structures and policies have tended to reinforce old models and traditional ways of working. The latter reflects resilient departmental silos and the associated policy silos that are in turn supported by budgetary processes. Equally, the capacity of civil society by itself to tackle many of these issues is constrained by a lack of capital, skills and resources to take promising ideas to scale (Ibid).

Murray *et al.* (2010) observe that new paradigms tend to flourish in areas where the institutions are most open to them, and where the forces of the old are weak. They argue that this can be seen more in innovations around self-management of diseases and public health than around hospitals, in public participation than parliaments, and in innovation around active ageing than pension provision. In addition, much of this innovation points towards a new kind of economy—the 'social economy'—characterised by distributed networks to manage relationships (and supported by broadband, mobile and other means of communication), as well as blurred boundaries between production and consumption, and an emphasis on collaboration, and strong values. Social innovation can thus take place "inside or outside of public services. It can be developed by the public, private or third sectors, or users and communities – and equally, some innovation developed by these sectors does not qualify as social innovation because it does not directly address major social challenges" (Harris and Albury 2009:11-12). The concept is often used to describe social entrepreneurship and social enterprises, but it is much broader than both of these – although it may overlap with one or the other or both. This chapter discusses social innovation in the health field in Ireland and the overlapping fields of the social economy, social entrepreneurship and social enterprise. It explores the institutions which promote innovation (funds, agencies, and intermediaries) and the enabling conditions, categorised by Murray *et al.* (2010:9) as the "public sector, the grant economy of civil society, the private sector, and the household", as they relate to social innovation in health in the 21st century.

The Context for Social Innovation in Health in Ireland
Healthcare in Ireland is deeply rooted in the social economy, from the philanthropist efforts which led to the first hospitals in the early 18th century, to the array of services provided by religious orders in the 19th century, and the state provisions that continue to serve as the conduit to independent service providers in the 21st century. Today, the Health Services Executive (the HSE) supports some 1,908 organisations across a wide range of bodies, some small, others very large, with Section 39 grants[47] amounting to €538,537,508 in 2015 (McInerney and Finn 2015). Organisations in receipt of funding above €250,000 are divided into a series of 'care groups' categorised as: disability; older persons; mental health; social inclusion; drug task force; palliative care chronic illness; primary care and health/wellbeing. Additionally, the HSE also provides grant funding to non-statutory bodies under Section 38 of the 2004

---

[47] This provision has been maintained to date and is contained in the 2004 Health Act (contained in Section 39) and applications administered by the newly established 32 Local Health Offices (Harvey 2007).

Health Act[48]. On paper, the two are difficult to distinguish between but in practice, they often fund organisations of comparable size and function and the reasons why some organisations are funded under Section 38 and others under Section 39 are neither clear nor transparent, even to some HSE officials (Ibid). Section 38 funds a smaller number of larger organisations - between 40 and 50 - largely in the acute hospital and disability sectors, amounting to €202,222,934,069 in 2015.

The Social Economy and Health Field in Ireland
While Ireland's social economy can be seen to include charities, co-operatives, voluntary associations and non-profits, the label is not widely used to collectively describe them and many organisations do not identify themselves with the social economy, or even fully understand the term (O'Shaughnessy and O'Hara 2016). The term 'social enterprise' is more readily recognisable, having entered the public policy discourse in the 1990s with the European policy agenda around job creation and social inclusion. Yet to date there is no commonly agreed definition of social enterprise, largely because social enterprises take various legal forms from country to country and are engaged in a wide range of activities from provision of healthcare and housing to care and work insertion (The Young Foundation 2012). In 2013, Forfás, the advisory body to the Irish government on enterprise policy, proposed a definition which is similar to international definitions "...an enterprise that trades for a social/societal purpose, where at least part of its income is earned from its trading activity, is separate from government and where the surplus is primarily reinvested in the social objective" (Forfás 2013:22). Economically the sector is of growing interest to government, with responsibility for its development now resting under the Department for Arts, Heritage, Regional, Rural and Gaeltacht Affairs, and the first National Policy on

---

[48] The origins of Section 38 can be traced to Section 26 of the Health Act, 1970 which repealed Section 10 of the Health Act 1953. The 1970 act states: 26. — (1) 'A health board may, in accordance with such conditions (which may include provision for superannuation) as may be specified by the Minister, make and carry out an arrangement with a person or body to provide services under the Health Acts, 1947 to 1970, for persons eligible for such services' (Department of Health, 1970).

Social Enterprise expected to be published later in the year (Dáil Éireann Debates 2017).

There is limited evidence available on the number of social enterprises in Ireland. The Forfás report notes there were 1,420 social enterprises in Ireland in 2009, employing over 25,000 people, with a combined income of around €1.4 billion. This figure is however disputed in an EU report which argues it is not based on any particular definition of a social enterprise, but rather derived from the number of enterprises registered on a non-profit business database in 2009, which includes both companies limited by guarantee and registered charities (ICF Consulting 2014). The EU report argues that well over half of these organisations do not generate any revenues from trading activity (based on the application of the EU operational definition[49]) and therefore the number of social enterprises in this group is around 520[50]. The Forfás report also provides limited disaggregation of social enterprise activities. It notes that one third of social enterprises are in childcare and other areas include the arts, tourism, social housing/ accommodation, social services, and environmental services, with almost one third of enterprises characterised as 'multi-functional' but provides no further disaggregation.

Similarly, there is no single database of social entrepreneurs in Ireland and no national business surveys that include

---

[49] The European Commission defines a social enterprise as "an operator in the social economy whose main objective is to have a social impact rather than make a profit for their owners or shareholders. It operates by providing goods and services for the market in an entrepreneurial and innovative fashion and uses its profits primarily to achieve social objectives. It is managed in an open and responsible manner and, in particular, involves employees, consumers and stakeholders affected by its commercial activities" (Communication from the Commission 2011/682 final).

[50] The European report notes that organisations that might self-identify as social enterprises include: companies limited by guarantee, friendly societies, credit unions, and industrial and provident societies (the most usual legal form of cooperatives). In terms of the 1,420 companies limited by guarantee and registered as charities, around 520 carried economic activities (i.e. had revenues from trading); 48 organisation were registered as friendly societies, of which some might be considered social enterprises; credit unions distribute profits to their members and there is no profit cap, hence it is unlikely that there are social enterprises in this group; industrial and provident societies (e.g. cooperatives) are unlikely to meet the social enterprise criterion on profit and asset distribution (ICF Consulting 2014).

questions about social enterprise or social entrepreneurs. Social entrepreneurs are individuals who are involved in creating new social ventures or finding creative ways of using underused assets (The Young Foundation 2012), they are individuals who come up with ideas for social ventures, combining doing good with doing well. In Ireland, they are encouraged through groups such as Social Entrepreneurs Ireland and the Social Innovation Fund through mentoring and monetary support. Aside from information compiled from sector stakeholders and such like, evidence on the social economy relies on academic research studies, providing no more than a snapshot of a point in time (Forfás 2013). In addition, comparisons between studies are made more difficult due to differences in methodologies and interpretation of sectoral activities. With this in mind, the following section provides the context for policy developments, followed by examples of social innovations in healthcare and a discussion on the barriers and opportunities for the social economy in healthcare.

Policy Developments

Since the 1990s, Ireland's social economy has been strongly shaped by European policy and in particular by efforts to create alternative models of production and consumption to support organisations engaged in work integration activities and the social inclusion of disadvantaged groups (Edmiston 2015). In 1993, the European Commission published a White Paper on Growth, Competitiveness and Employment, highlighting the problem of structural unemployment and social exclusion within EU member states. The White Paper identified the potential for new jobs in the 'third sector' or social economy to help address unmet needs in disadvantaged communities. In Ireland, the Department of Enterprise, Trade & Employment created the Social Economy Programme (SEP) in 1999 to provide employment grants to support the development of the social economy in disadvantaged communities[51]. In 2003, an

---

[51] Employment grants were administered by FÁS, the national body responsible for education and training. In 2013, FÁS was replaced by SOLAS, the new State organisation with responsibility for funding, planning and co-ordinating Further Education and Training (FET) in Ireland.

evaluation of the SEP found that the overall package of support was inadequate for the development of social economy enterprises due to a narrow pool of skilled labour, limited formal involvement of relevant statutory bodies and the incapacity of the targeted markets to support sustainability (WRC 2003). In 2007, it was replaced by a new funding programme, the Community Services Programme (CSP).

The new CSP strengthened the association of social enterprises with locally based community development, but funding was not tied to sustainability, and so a very significant number of organisations supported by the CSP were consequently found to be heavily reliant on public funding. O'Shaughnessy and O'Hara (2016) argue such organisations are not enterprise driven, but rather are conduits for state funding programmes. They argue that both the CSP and its predecessor the SEP demonstrate the labour market integration approach adopted by successive Irish governments towards the development of Ireland's social economy, pointing out that the social enterprises that have emerged from this type of state support are typically engaged in community service provision and labour market integration. This assertion is also supported by evidence of the continued work integration focus of the Community Employment scheme (CE) first introduced in 1994 and maintained in the new Social Inclusion and Community Activation Programme (SICAP) introduced in 2015. While both CE schemes and the SICAP support social enterprise, they are primarily concerned with employment activation. A report by McGuinness, Bergin, and Whelan (2016) confirms that two-thirds of training places under the SICAP have been in the area of employment. Similarly, the Wage Subsidy Scheme (WSS) offers financial support for employers who employ people with registered disabilities; and the European LEADER programme and the social enterprise measure of the Dormant Accounts Fund are both concerned with addressing employment inclusion through jobs creation in delivering services to disadvantaged communities. This includes employment to support the growing needs of an ageing population, rising dependency ratios and a smaller productive population which threaten the affordability and sustainability of public budgets for social policies (Communication from the Commission to the European

Parliament, the Council, the European Economic and Social Committee and the Committee of the Regions 2013). The focus on job creation was reinforced by the economic recession of 2008-2012 which contributed to the European debt crisis, increasing unemployment and decreasing tax revenues, further challenging the sustainability of member states' social protection systems.

Types of Social Innovation in Healthcare

Policy goals to create greater integration of services, greater efficiency and more personalisation are evident in many of the social innovations in healthcare. The drive towards the personalisation of services and a whole person approach is particularly evident in the disability sector. Transforming Lives – the programme to implement the recommendations of the 'Value for money and policy review of disability services in Ireland' (Department of Health 2012) is, for example, currently driving the implementation of national policy which aims to introduce personal budgets for people with disabilities. Personal budgets, which can take a number of forms including direct payment to the individual, are used in a number of countries and have been piloted in Ireland since 2012. A government appointed taskforce on personalised budgets for people with disabilities is due to report to the Minister of State with special responsibility for disabilities before the end of 2017. The taskforce will advise the Minister on the best options for personal budget, changing how disability services are funded and provided, shifting choice and control from professionals and administrators to the individual with a disability and their family.

Social innovation can also be seen to involve new ways of delivering services designed to foster greater efficiency and effectiveness, especially through information and communication technologies for health. More commonly known as 'eHealth', this is healthcare that is supported by mobile devices, such as mobile phones, patient monitoring devices, personal digital assistants and other wireless devices. In 2013, the Department of Health published Ireland's eHealth Strategy which sees digital solutions as key to achieving the integration of care and the removal of false boundaries. To date, eHealth solutions have been piloted in a number of areas, for example, in the treatment of haemophilia, enabling this illness to be managed, controlled and audited digitally in the patient's home by using the patient's mobile phone, a development that has been warmly welcomed by the Irish Haemophilia Society. It is estimated that the reduction in the need for drugs from better monitoring of people with haemophilia represents a saving of around €10 million a year (Committee on the Future of Healthcare 2016). Likewise, in the treatment of epilepsy, the genomics sequencing programme with the Royal College of Surgeons in Ireland is working to identify the genome of suspected epilepsy patients. With as many as 130 epilepsy-related deaths in Ireland each year, 90 of which are considered to be undiagnosed children, the cost of finding the correct medicines for those patients is estimated to be in the region of €5 million a year (Ibid). Investment in genomics sequencing aims to make treatment available for 40,000 people with epilepsy in Ireland, with treatment personalised to their type of epilepsy. Plans are also being made to move to a single digital lab system to facilitate electronic ordering, tests and results and to share these between acute, primary and community care settings to reduce the burden of testing and retesting and to achieve financial savings to the State. The timing of all of this will, of course, depend on available resources and the chief information officer for the HSE has advised the Oireachtas of his 'very lean team' in comparison to other government departments and health care systems, with just one IT person supporting every 236 people in the HSE compared to other departments where there is one IT person supporting every 11 resources (Committee on the Future of Healthcare 2016). Currently the HSE allocate 1% of its budget to digital solutions compared to an average EU budget for eHealth of over 3% (Ibid).

A good example of a social innovation based on eHealth is the MyMind Centre for mental well-being. MyMind is a not-for-profit organisation developed in response to the mental health needs of low-income populations associated with access issues. Evidence shows long delays in accessing services are associated with poorer outcomes for service users (The King's Fund 2015), with relatively minor issues often escalating by the time referrals are made. The MyMind Centre offers fast and affordable access to professionals using a self-referral model and online services. There are two MyMind offices in Dublin, one in Cork and one in Limerick and a variety of experienced therapists are available at each location or alternatively services can be accessed online. The waiting time for an appointment is no more than 72 hours and a referral from a doctor is not required. Direct access is available using a low-call number or via the MyMind website. People who are unemployed and students are charged €20 for services, subsidised by profits from fee-paying clients. Services are provided by a panel of around 50 mental health professionals, including psychologists, psychotherapists, counsellors and life coaches, who receive an allowance for their time. Like many social innovations, MyMind developed at the grassroots, local level and grew from the bottom up. Initially supported by grant funding from Social Entrepreneurs Ireland (SEI), its founder is now a recognised Ashoka Fellow and his solution a 'System-Changing Idea for Health', considered a highly scalable social franchise model (Forfás 2013).

Ashoka is an international association of social entrepreneurs (Ashoka Fellows) promoting social innovation in America, Asia, Africa and the Middle East, Europe and (since 2007) Ireland. Ashoka Fellows, of which there are currently 13 in Ireland, receive living stipends and pro-bono resources to develop their social innovation models. In addition to supporting local innovations like MyMind, Ashoka support international Fellows to localise their solutions in Ireland, as in the case of 'Siel Bleu'. Jean Michel Richard became an Ashoka fellow with his Siel Bleu solution in 2006, which started in Strasbourg in 1997, after he recognized the importance of physical activity as a preventative health tool for older adults. Evidence shows sedentary behaviour increases the risk of ill health, including being overweight and obesity, and is associated with metabolic diseases. Critically, over two thirds (67%) of the older population have been found to be sedentary for 8.5 hours per day (Harvey, Chastin, and Skelton 2013). Siel Bleu started as a six month pilot programme in 12 nursing homes in Strasbourg. Today, they work with over 3,000 nursing homes in France on a weekly basis and the service has expanded into Belguim, Spain and more recently to Ireland when Ashoka helped to localise the service. Siel Bleu Ireland was established in 2011 as a social enterprise company specialising in physical activities for older adults. Today they work with over 1,650 people on a weekly basis across 16 counties in both the community, and in nursing homes. They operate on the basis of user charges; nursing homes are charged between €49 and €55 per session, and community groups are charged €4 per person. Over the next three years, they hope to achieve sustainability by growing their service to over 225 nursing homes, around half of all nursing homes in Ireland (Change Makers 2015).

Most social enterprises in Ireland are small, with around one third reporting an annual turnover of less than €100,000, and 60% reporting an annual turnover of less than €300,000 (ICF Consulting 2014), which in turn can lead to sustainability challenges especially in a highly competitive market, as discussed below. One exception to this is Rehab Enterprises, the commercial division of The Rehab Group in Ireland[52]. A case study of Rehab Enterprises by Forfás (2013) shows that it is positioned at the farthest economic end of the continuum of any social enterprise in Ireland, working with businesses in a range of areas, including recycling, logistics, retail services and disability consultancy in four European countries, employing over 530 people of whom over 313 have a disability. It has 1,800 active customers in Ireland, including most of the large multinational companies and competes with other commercial for-profit entities in all market areas it serves. The only support Rehab Enterprises receives other than its commercially earned income is the WSS. It is the largest creator of jobs under the WSS in Ireland, although the WSS contribution represents less than 7% of its income (Ibid).

CareBright, formerly known as the Rural Community Care Network (RCCN) represents another exception. The RCCN was set up as a company limited by guarantee in 1999 when it was awarded funding from FÁS under the Community Employment (CE) scheme to deliver a visitation service to older people and people with disabilities in the Ballyhoura area in Limerick. Curtis (2013) provides a detailed account of the development of the company, pointing out that when it started, there were no

---

[52] The Rehab Group is a not-for-profit organisation for people with a disability. In Ireland, the Rehab Group incorporates the National Learning Network, RehabCare and Rehab Enterprises.

competitors in the market. After successfully applying to FÁS in 2002 to become part of the SEP, a new company called RCCNCL (Rural Community Care Network Caring Ltd.) was set up at the request of FÁS to run a social economy project across a wider area. RCCN Caring Ltd. evolved as an independent entity with a separate board of directors and become a registered provider for the HSE in 2006. After this, it grew quickly as a result of participation in the home-care package, continued grant assistance under the CSP and use of CE scheme participants who were paid for by the state the company gained money by charging for their services. Turnover went from just over half a million in 2005 to almost €4m in 2011. However, a series of events caused the company serious financial difficulties in 2011/12. In 2010, they lost a source of revenue when the board decided to break from the CE scheme and, added to this, the more successful the company became in terms of increasing its turnover and retained reserves, the more it found its grant aid from the CSP was cut back by the intermediary body, Pobal (Ibid). To compound matters, the HSE initiated a new procurement framework for home care services in 2011 designed to promote a more standardised and cost effective approach to provision. Few not-for-profit organisations were successful in gaining contracts, including RCCNCL. Out of 100 applicants nationally, only five were in the not-for-profit sector (Curtis 2013). It was at this stage that the company rebranded, becoming 'Carebright' in 2012, adopting a more commercial focus and guided by a new board with members with commercial business skills (O'Shaughnessy and O' Hara 2013). Carebright now provides a broader range of services which includes dementia care, 24 hour care, respite and post-operative care in the home, which may be covered by health insurance companies and training. They have also developed a professional website, a data-base for staff planning and acquired the Q mark. More recently, they undertook a capital built project to create Ireland's first dementia hub at a cost €4.85 million, funded by the Department of Health, the JP McManus Foundation with support from the Social Innovation Fund and CareBright's own cash reserves. The hub, which is expected to open in September 2017, plans to attract residents under the Nursing Homes Support Scheme, which provides financial support from the state for those who need long-term nursing home care, with residents making a contribution towards the cost of their care, and the state paying the balance. The case of Rehab and Carebright highlight the changing face of the Irish not for profit sector and how the sector has been forced to incorporate market values in order to survive. In the case of Carebright, the work integration social enterprise model succumbed to the pressures of 'institutional isomorphism' as the company was forced to respond to other [private sector] organisations in the field by developing similar services to the for-profit sector and re-brand itself to increase its legitimacy with the HSE, private providers and potential future customers (Curtis 2013). While the introduction of EU public tendering requirement has opened up the home care market, it is forcing non-profit providers to taken on some of the characteristics of a private provider. A key challenge for the sector is therefore how to maintain a balance between operating like a for-profit organisation while at the same time retaining not for profit values.

In Ireland, the public sector publishes more than 7,000 tenders each year with a combined worth of €9 billion and the HSE is responsible for around €4 billion of this (Corrigan and O Beirne 2014). Tenders for HSE contracts can run into several millions of euros and attract at least five submissions per tender, so margins between successful and unsuccessful tenders are extremely tight. Records from the Bid Management Service for 2014 show there were 40,000 submissions made by 20,000 bidders for centralised purchasing in the Office for Government Procurements (OGP), which in addition to the HSE includes Defence, Local Government and Education (Brennan 2014). More importantly, only 10% of these bids were from SMEs. According to the Bid Management Service, one of the main reasons for this is that most SMEs do not understand the basic rules of public procurement (Ibid). This reflects the relatively small size of social enterprises and their inexperience. Public contracts tend to be large and attract interest from large organisations with access to the technical skills and experience required to prepare a winning bid. This is compounded by contracts granted to providers from outside Ireland, leading to calls to create a more supportive infrastructure of Irish social enterprises. This includes a call to raise the threshold for publishing tenders from €25,000 to the prevailing EU thresholds and for all contracts below these thresholds to be reserved for Irish small businesses registered on eTenders or for bid consortiums involving small businesses (Brennan 2016). In addition, a call to compensate for or modify public funding criteria to ensure that social enterprises can access equivalent financial resources, creating a level playing field between social enterprises and mainstream micro, small and medium enterprises for access to funding (Hynes 2016) and by providing more support for training, mentoring, and business development (Forfás 2013; Brennan 2016). In addition, plans are at an advanced stage to address the absence in procurement guidelines of a social value clause, which other European countries have included in their procurement legislation. Social value clauses are designed to improve access to public procurement by adding social considerations in contract requirements. Section 3 of the Public Services and Procurement (Social Value) Bill 2017, currently going through the Dáil, deals with the community benefits requirements and sets out how a social value clause would work. It will require a state body, local authority or department issuing a tender to take into account the benefits of awarding the contract to the local and national economy when assessing bids.

The impending introduction of a social value clause into public procurement requirements in Ireland is broadly welcomed although some tensions remain, e.g. in relation to differences in pay and conditions between staff employed in Section 38 and Section 39 organisations, which is not addressed in the Bill. A debate in the Seanad heard how staff in Section 38 organisations, which are found largely in the acute hospital and disability sectors, are classified as public servants and are subject to the standard salary scales for the health sector, as well as having public service pension schemes and are counted in public service employment numbers (Seanad Éireann Debate 2013). By contrast, employees of agencies that receive grant-aid from the HSE under Section 39 are not public servants and are not specifically subject to the pay scales approved for public servants (Ibid). There have been calls for staff in Section 39 funded organisations to progress onto scales comparable with their counterparts in Section 38 funded organisation, and for

128

Section 39 of the 2004 Health Act to be replaced with group and sector specific funding mechanisms (McInerney and Finn 2015). A further problem concerns the vast range of non-statutory organisations funded by the HSE. According to an annual report for 2016 (HSE 2016), some 2,300 non-statutory agencies received funding in 2016, and 9 agencies received [S.38] over 50% of the funding available for all non-statutory agencies. The vast range of organisations funded under Section 39 has led to duplication of, and gaps in, services e.g. several groups deal with almost identical mental health issues, some 124 groups work in older people's services and 109 organisations work in the disability sector (Jones 2016). Questions which have been raised relate to value for money of charitable organisations in Ireland, particularly in light of a surge of controversies and scandals since 2013, ranging from revelations about exorbitant executive pay and 'top-ups' to suspected fraud.

Innovative Solutions to Fund, Deliver and Scale.
The need for social innovation in healthcare is clear. We face critical challenges in developing integrated care, compounded by capacity constraints across the system, including waiting lists and emergency department overcrowding. In August 2016, there were 2,080 children and adolescents waiting to be seen by the Child and Adolescent Mental Health Services, with 170 waiting for more than 12 months (HSE 2016). Healthcare has been especially vulnerable to cuts imposed in the wake of the global economic crisis, with almost half (43%) of all public sector human resource cuts made in the health service, and a moratorium on recruitment and a targeted voluntary early retirement scheme (HSE 2016). Acknowledgement by policymakers that global challenges of contemporary societies are both economic and social, with unstainable cost implications for modern welfare states, has led to a growing interest in social innovation as a policy intervention. The OECD (Organisation for Economic Cooperation and Development 2015) support new models of public and private partnership to fund, deliver and scale innovative solutions from the ground up e.g. social impact bonds (SIB) which bring together the public, private and voluntary sectors to solve big societal challenges by adopting a type of payment by results.

The SIB is a fixed-term bond based on a contract with a public body that agrees to pay for social outcomes and repayments by the contracting authority to investors dependant on the outcomes achieved. Interest in social impact bond (SIBs) has grown over recent years as a mechanism to address a range of entrenched social problems that governments have struggled to address, including children in care, homelessness, youth unemployment or long-term health issues. Countries such as the US, Belgium, the Netherlands, Portugal, Australia and the UK are piloting different variations of SIBs. According to the UK Cabinet Office, Essex County Council was the first local authority in the UK to commission a SIB (Cabinet Office n.d.). After creating a partnership with Children's Support Services Ltd, the council introduced a programme to improve the outcomes for 380 young people and their families on the edge of care or custody. The SIB was generated by different investors including Big Society Capital and Bridges Ventures, providing £3.1m to Children's Support Services Ltd. A special purpose vehicle was set up to manage the project. The Children's Support Services Ltd provides operational funding to the service provider (Action for Children), with payments back to investors coming from Essex County Council when outcomes are achieved (Ibid). The SIB enables the council to provide specialist therapy to improve parenting skills and family relationships to enable families to manage future crisis situations, therapy to 380 young people at risk of entering care and their families over an 8 year period. The primary outcome metric is the average number of care days saved compared to the average number of care days spent in care by a comparable group of children over a 30-month period. The value of outcome payments per-care-placement-days-saved corresponds to a share of the cost to the local authority of care placement for this group of young people and, with the cost of care placement ranging from £20,000 to £180,000 per year per individual, reductions in placements offer significant savings. Investors are expected to earn between 8-12% annual interest on their investment (Ibid).

In Ireland, the 2011 programme for government contained a commitment to introduce SIBs, with two projects subsequently selected for piloting: 'moving homeless families into permanent housing' and 'improving outcomes for young people remanded on bail'. A report by the Irish Governmental Economic Evaluation Service (IGEES) found that the SIB had provided impetus for improved outcomes in the homeless pilot, but adds that results were achieved without the full application of the social impact investment model. The second pilot did not progress because a feasibly study suggested it was not suitable for SIB (IGEES 2015). It found that SIBs can result in significant additional administrative costs being incurred, with considerable legal and financial complexities to consider in addition to large initial fixed costs for training commissioning staff, engaging specialist expertise and working with service providers (Ibid). It concludes that scale will help ensure that value for money is achieved by spreading the cost over a large number of projects.

While few SIBs have been applied to healthcare, evidence suggests this is likely to evolve, for example, the advisory group set up to examine the potential for social impact investment in Ireland recommended investment in a number of health care areas. This included: the management of chronic conditions in the community based on the use of the Patient Journey Tracking System to track older people discharged from hospital with chronic conditions to reduce re-admission and delay the need for residential care; early intervention in dementia; and an exercise and education programme to improve the balance, well-being, risk of falls and hospital admissions in people with MS. In addition, in 2016 the Minister of State at the Department of Health in Ireland indicated his department was examining the feasibility of utilising SIBs as a funding model to improve both treatment and rehabilitation service outcomes and that the outcome of this work would be used to inform decisions as to the viability of SIBs in maximising the social benefits which the new national drugs strategy seeks to achieve (Dáil Éireann Debates 2016).

Conclusion
This chapter has shown how the social economy can support better healthcare. It has also shown the critically important role of social entrepreneurs in driving change and the organisations that can help scale up initiatives. In addition, a small number of social enterprises have successfully adopted a business model to

achieve sustainability, positioned themselves somewhere along the economic spectrum in order to generate sufficient resources and maintain a low dependence on external funding. Their challenge going forward is how to maintain the balance between operating like a for profit organisation whilst at the same time retaining not for profit values in an increasingly competitive market. For the most part however, social enterprises in Ireland will remain relatively small and economically vulnerable. Government and policy makers can facilitate the spread of innovation in health among smaller providers e.g. by creating a level playing field between social enterprises and mainstream micro, small and medium enterprises for access to funding and by providing more support for training, mentoring, and business development. In addition, the potential for new funding mechanisms in the form of SIB provides opportunities for the non-statutory sector in general and social enterprise sector in particular, to move away from dependency on grant and wage subsidisation to a situation where they have a greater incentive to produce, trade, generate revenue and reinvest surpluses (Hynes 2016).

The EU Commissioner for Employment and Social Affairs (Marianne Thyssen, 1st December 2016) recently announced EU plans to significantly increase the funds available to member states to develop favourable conditions for social economy and social enterprises. Together with the European Social Fund, this will be supported through new grant agreements with organisations promoting social investment markets in member states through the Social Impact Investment Instruments under the European Fund for Strategic Investment. These instruments, focussing on Incubators, Business Angels, and Payment by results schemes such as SIBs, are designed to boost social investment markets and provide new opportunities for social enterprises in Europe to start-up and scale-up (Ibid). In addition, the European fund for strategic investment in employment and social Innovation is to be used to increase the scale of financial instruments for social enterprises and microfinance. The total amount of support to these areas is expected to increase from 193 million euros under the Employment and Social Innovation programme to about 1 billion euros (Ibid). To conclude on an optimistic note, with the opportunity for new funding mechanisms beckoning and a new 'National Policy on Social Enterprise' due shortly, Ireland's social economy may be about to take an important leap forward.

CHAPTER 10
SOCIAL INNOVATION AND EDUCATION

Thomas Murray and Farah Mohktareizadeh

Introduction
Set in the year 2157, Isaac Asimov's short story, 'The Fun They Had', tells of eleven-year-old Margie, whose neighbour Tommy discovers a real book. Since both children learn individually at home using a mechanical teacher, Margie is surprised to discover that the book recounts a time when children learned together in large schools. (They even had a real person for a teacher!) After some initial scepticism, by the end of the story Margie daydreams about what it must have been like and 'the fun they had' (Asimov 2017 [1951]). For Asimov's contemporary readers, long habituated to mass schooling, the story's message is perhaps conservative: 'things could be worse'. Today's readers, readily familiar with social media and communication online, might more readily identify with the story's warning about learning becoming an isolated, solitary, and ultimately dehumanising experience. Equally, however, the possibilities for connection and learning afforded by an interconnected world are far greater than those imaginable even a generation ago.

Today, the key technical and political challenge for those attempting socially innovative forms of education remains that of combining technology with human empathy in such a way that both communities and individual learners can flourish and fulfil their potential. In this chapter, we map the contours of social innovation and community education in Ireland. We begin by outlining the social challenge of educational inequality in Ireland today. In particular, specific challenges and opportunities for education are presented in an age of rapid digital disruption and marked digital division. We then present a case-study in social innovation seeking to address these challenges. Launched in 2016, An Cosán Virtual Community College is a social enterprise set up to scale the work of An Cosán, a community education centre that has served the community of Tallaght West for over thirty years. An Cosán VCC utilises a blended online learning model to provide a wide variety of introductory and higher education programmes to learners and communities throughout the island of Ireland. VCC demonstrates the potential of harnessing 21st century learning technologies to a community education ethos to empower learners and their communities.

We underestimate the promise of genuine community education at our cost (Thompson 1997; Connolly 2003). Today's prevailing global educational discourses and actions, shaped by the World Bank, the OECD, the WTO and UNESCO, narrow the purpose of learning to best serve economic utility (Spring 2008; Ryan 2016). In Ireland, these pressures intensified following the 2008 economic crisis. A range of measures, including austerity cuts, tuition increases, increased managerialism, and corporatisation, served to bolster neoliberal discipline within the education system (Lynch 2014). Increasingly, state funding requirements are a key mechanism for marginalising emancipatory forms of community learning in favour of learning for credentials or labour activation (AONTAS 2011:121). Given these circumstances, it is worth restating that credentials and employment do not exhaust the purposes of education. Education is intrinsically valuable to individual, community, and societal development, enriching our shared fabric of cultural, social, political and economic life. On this view, education is not a personal commodity but a shared human right. The stakes in this debate remain high. Communities and individuals will either design their future learning, or have it designed for them as part of another's vision.

The Social Challenge of Educational Inequality
Since the 1980s, neoliberal capitalism has facilitated widening global inequality (Harvey 2007). Today, the world's richest eight people control more wealth than the poorest 3.5 billion. OECD predictions suggest inequality rising further by 40% by 2050 (Mason 2015:x). In unequal societies such as ours, education is increasingly a competition for advantage (Marsh 2011). Those privileged with material and cultural capital can and will use it to ensure advantages accrue to their children within schools and universities. Wealthier parents are enabled to subsidise their children privately through fees, grinds, tutoring, trips, summer camps, IT supports, and so forth (Lynch 2014). Worse still, the education system can transform these 'inequalities of fact' into

'inequalities of merit', thereby legitimating an unequal competition for advantage while persuading those whom it eliminates that their social destiny is due to their lack of 'natural gifts' (Bourdieu 2008). Well-resourced public education services can offset these inequalities to varying degrees. In particular, 'equitable access to higher education is a core part of the social contract and essential to ensuring that higher education delivers maximally for our economy and society' (Cassells 2015:7).

In Ireland, social inequality is registered and reproduced at all levels of the education system. Notwithstanding state commitments to 'free' education, school costs for primary and secondary school children are often three to four times more than the public supports provided, with one in ten parents compelled to go into debt to afford them (Barnardos 2016). Social class further impacts on children's educational attainment. At the end of primary school, children from higher professional backgrounds had a mean literacy score of 43 (out of a possible 50), those from semi- or un-skilled manual backgrounds had a score of 28, and those in households where neither parent was employed had a mean score of 25 (Smyth and McCoy 2009:7). State examinations at junior and leaving certificate levels crystallise these differences. Each year, some 4,500 young people stop attending school before they complete their junior cert. Taking into account involuntary part-time work, and workers marginally attached to the labour market, Ireland has one of the largest rates of youth who are neither in employment nor in education' (OECD Economic Survey 2013, cited in Lynch 2014).

Class inequalities further manifest in unequal access to higher education. Higher education has witnessed a rapid expansion in Ireland, expanding six-fold over the last four decades (Fleming 2013:35). The tertiary attainment rate, at 52.3% in 2015, is well above the EU average (EU Commission 2017:41). However, this expansion has primarily occurred among 18 to 21 year olds and among those drawn from professional and managerial classes (Fleming 2013:35). Expansion has not significantly reduced glaring inequalities of access, notably, the under-representation of poorer socio-economic groups or mature students. Targets were set in 2008 that 3% and 20% of full-time new entrants would be from these two groups respectively by 2013; but rates of only 21% and 14% were achieved (Cassells 2015:22). Comparatively speaking, the degree of equity that characterises access to higher education in Ireland has been described as 'above average but well behind best practice' (Cassells 2015:22). The implications are very unevenly experienced and the gap remains pronounced: some 99% of Dublin 6 students will progress to higher education programmes compared to 15% in Dublin 15 (HEA 2014).

The specific barriers facing people accessing further and higher education in Ireland are varied and intersectional. They include financial cost, childcare considerations, geography, public transport availability, and lack of institutional access (HEA 2013). Moreover, these barriers remain operative for those learners who succeed in accessing higher education. Those parts of the higher education sector that have the largest proportions of disadvantaged and mature students (QQI Level 6 and 7 programmes in the Institutes of Technology) currently have the least success in retaining them: their non-progression rates are more than 3 times higher than those in Level 8 university programmes (Cassells 2015:39).

Recent austerity measures reinforced barriers to higher education and simultaneously undermined community-based supports and development initiatives. Higher education experienced a 25% fall in public funding during the economic recession (Department of Education and Skills 2016a). Ireland's spending on education and skills, at 4.3% of GDP in 2014, remains somewhat below the EU average of 4.9%. The EU Commission has warned that 'fairness and inclusion' are a concern, and that funding for appropriate strategies may prove 'insufficient' (EU Commission 2017:41). While tuition fees have yet to be re-introduced, registration fees remain a significant cost: students whose families are on very average or low incomes must pay fees of €2,500 per year (Lynch 2014). New entrants under the Back to Education Allowance (benefitting the disabled, lone parents and the unemployed) no longer receive maintenance support, making it almost impossible for those mature students on low incomes, or those with young children who need childcare, to return to third-level education (Lynch 2014). Austerity impacted particularly severely among the most marginalised groups in Irish society. Cuts of 80% to Traveller-specific supports occurred notwithstanding compelling evidence that Travellers are among the most educationally disadvantaged groups in Ireland (Harvey 2013). Similarly, asylum seekers surviving in direct provision centres cannot access higher education due to the prohibitive costs of non-EU student fees, averaging four times more than those of Irish/EU learners. The educational inequality reinforced by these austerity measures may yet be compounded by the wave of digital disruption now upon us.

Educational Inequality in an Age of Digital Disruption

We are living through an exciting period of technological innovation. Highlights of the past twenty-five years include the launch of eBay (1997), the first wifi-enabled laptop (1999), the rollout of broadband internet (2000), and the expansion of 3G telecoms (2001). A wave of standardised applications and digital tools, dubbed Web 2.0, arrived thereafter. These included the launch of social networks such as MySpace (2003), Facebook (2004) and Twitter (2006), followed by the launch of the iPhone (2007) and Android phone (2009) as well as the rapid rise of e-book publishing. The next ten years will occasion the rollout of billions of intelligent machine-to-machine connections, dubbed the 'Internet of Things' (Mason 2015:125; Dyer-Witherford 2015:92-3). The digital disruption brought about by information technology has ushered in startling social transformations, at least three of which will impact significantly on the future of education and educational equality.

First, automation is likely to displace much human labour. Some 47% of all current jobs in the US are susceptible to automation over the next twenty years, notably those in transportation and logistics, office and administration support, and labour production (Mason 2015:140). Parenthetically, in the face of North America and Europe's slow recovery from recession, the most common proposal for dealing with the effects of automation on employment is more education: "as if this could summon corporate investment in human capital, rather than just intensify competition for what jobs exist" (Dyer-Witherford 2015:184). Second, information goods corrode market mechanisms to form prices correctly. In short, markets are based on scarcity while information is abundant, pushing the cost of reproducing information goods towards zero (Romer 1990). Increasingly, information goods are either free, or have very limited commercial value. Third, we are seeing the rise of collaborative production, the appearance of goods, services and organisational forms that no longer respond to the dictates of market signals or managerial hierarchies (see Dyer-Witherford 2015:91). Wikipedia – the most well-known example - is the biggest information product in the world, produced by 27,000 volunteers, for free, abolishing the encyclopaedia business and depriving advertisers of some $3 billion a year in revenue (Mason 2015:xv). These tendencies toward automation, abundance, and digital sharing are not inevitable but politically contested. All have important, underappreciated implications for education.

The digital disruption is reshaping the way we teach and learn. Within traditional 20th century school rooms, technologically enhanced learning currently presents opportunities for lowering the cost of education through online provision and cloud computing, for increasing accessibility to information for geographically disadvantaged learners, and for better including differently abled students through the provision of technological learning aids. But this is only the tip of the iceberg. The 21st century classroom is situated in a society where technology is pervasive and where learners, thanks to smart phones and tablets, are constantly online. Increasingly, schools may no longer even be located in a physical building, but thoroughly defused throughout society. Pedagogical relationships may shift from traditional 'teacher to student' instruction to the formation of collective 'webs of learning' (Leinonen *et al.* 2009), or group collaborations centred on 'pervasive connectivity' (Beetham 2013). In Ireland, higher education institutions have already made "great strides over the past five years towards integrating emerging technologies and strategies in teaching and learning" (NMC 2015). Key trends include the introduction of team-based approaches and the use of blended learning models, such as the flipped classroom and Bring Your Own Device initiatives (BYOD) (NMC 2015:2). These emerging technologies and strategies in teaching and learning are best understood in terms of a recurring conflict between two key educational models seeking to achieve different ends.

Hierarchical social formations typically favour the 'functionalist' educational model (Hicks 2004). Learning is generally understood to be an individual cognitive process, centred on imparting knowledge and skills deemed 'useful' according to the perceived requirements of economy and society. Success equates with learners acquiring standardised accreditations or certifications, necessary to compete successfully in the labour market. The digital disruption, however, presents specific challenges for the established functionalist model. Children starting school this September will probably retire sometime in the 2070s. The current pace of technological change means that state-run education systems are expected to equip and train learners for jobs that do not yet exist and are perhaps unimaginable at present (Puttnam 2015). Responding to this uncertainty, state and industry are seeking to create an agile labour force capable of finding niche employment in flexible, changing work environments (Boltanski and Chiapello 2005). Mass education systems that co-evolved with the industrial revolution look set to be challenged if not displaced by lifelong learning in post-industrial, knowledge societies. It is in this context that the OECD's educational prescriptions focus on skills and competencies, an approach which narrows curriculum to that which is measurable, while diminishing learning as a process of discovery and critical reflection (Ryan 2016:43).

Conversely, alternatives to the dominant, functionalist model of education might be characterised as 'emancipatory' or 'social action' models of education. Learning is understood here to be a socio-cultural process, centred on cultivating new knowledge through dialogue and self-reflection as well as on critically analysing and transforming social relations (Freire 2001; Leinonen *et al.* 2009). Equally, the 21st century classroom offers extraordinary possibilities for new forms of collaborative e-learning, including collaboration within a digital economy of share and share-alike. A recent experiment to set up a Wikiversity, for instance, centred around learners creating open educational resources, through co-planning and design of learning materials as well as online collaboration and publishing through web forums, blogs and wikis. The Wikiversity's founders had consciously looked to Scandinavia's established traditions of free adult and community education to co-create a virtual learning environment that clearly favoured participatory and co-creative learning over acquisitive or functionalist learning (Leinonen *et al.* 2009).

The capacity of learners, both individually and collectively, to meaningfully choose between these models and to flourish in a globally interconnected world is uneven. The digital divide refers to inequality regarding access to, use of, or impact of information and communications technologies (Norris 2001). The term recognises that access to digital information is not ubiquitous, but instead mirrors structural inequalities that already exist in society. The provision of infrastructure to ensure Internet connectivity, the development of digital literacy skills, and the capabilities of users to produce rather than consume content all vary considerably. Of a world population of some 7.3 billion people, 47% are Internet users. While over two-thirds of the world's 7.3 billion people live within an area covered by a mobile broadband network, only 47% use the Internet and significant differences in terms of broadband speeds and quality persist (ITU 2017). Similar structural inequalities, concerning digital access, literacy, and production capacity, persist within countries of the Global North.

In Ireland, the most significant challenge to the introduction of new educational technologies is the lack of sufficient institution resources and infrastructure (NMC 2015:3). More effort and resources are required to take advantage of even low-cost connectivity and digital storage solutions, such as cloud computing. Scaling educational technologies and improving digital literacy among teachers and students are further key challenges identified. These challenges correspond to the wider experience of the digital divide in Irish society. The disparity in broadband quality across the country is frequently described as a 'digital apartheid' (Burke-Kennedy 2017). The percentage of households able to access high-speed broadband in Ireland (82%) surpassed the EU average (76%), including in rural areas (50% of households compared to 40 % EU average) (European Commission 2017: 54). However, 7% of rural homes have no access to basic broadband (EU Commission 2017:54). Moreover, 35% of current subscriptions are below 30Mbps, the minimum threshold laid down in the National Broadband Plan (Burke-

Kennedy 2017). It is within these conditions of social inequality and transformation that a new social enterprise, An Cosán Virtual Community College, seeks to address the digital divide and educational disadvantage.

An Cosán Virtual Community College

An Cosán Virtual Community College emerged from over thirty years of shared experience in community education. Dr. Ann Louise Gilligan and Dr. Katherine Zappone founded the Shanty Education Project in 1986. Subsequently renamed An Cosán (or 'The Path'), the organisation moved to its current location, a purpose-built centre in Jobstown, in 1999 (An Cosán, 2006). The project's stated aim is to address poverty and disadvantage in the local community of Tallaght West through education. In the intervening years, An Cosán has offered long term education and training to over 5,000 adults, primarily those on low income or those otherwise prevented from accessing education, while promoting community enterprise and development. Currently, An Cosán facilitates some 600 students annually to access part-time education programmes, from basic literacy to degree level (An Cosán 2017).

The ethos and philosophy promoted by An Cosán recognises that the education system's barriers and failings have inscribed a deep distrust of formal education among many marginalised learners. Its ethos is consciously different, combining education for holistic personal development, for participation in the market, and for participation in a democratic society. Hospitality, providing 'a place of heart and home', is integral to An Cosán, recognising that learners' basic needs must be met before they can excel in their studies. Access to onsite accredited counsellors, qualified early years care practitioners, and academic mentors are available. This ethos informs pedagogical best practice: "We understand Community Education as education through dialogue where the participants' own experience, wisdom, and learning are deeply valued and respected. Learning in this context is reciprocal" (An Cosán 2006). Teaching spaces are comfortable and informal, offering learners every opportunity to participate in open and encouraging learning discussions. This ethos now informs a

142

pioneering virtual learning initiative to address educational disadvantage across Ireland.

Officially launched in 2016, An Cosán Virtual Community College (VCC) is a non-profit, social enterprise initiative which seeks to scale the social impact of An Cosán. Its core mission is to bring further and higher education to communities struggling with inequality and the injustice of poverty through a model of blended learning, combining face-to-face workshops with online teaching. VCC delivers programmes spanning the national framework of qualifications, ranging from unaccredited education to QQI level 7 degrees. These include basic courses such as 'Community Development' and 'Community Drugs Work' and higher education programmes such as 'Learning to Learn at Third Level', 'Community Leadership', 'Citizenship and Social Action' and 'Social Enterprise Development'. It also offers accredited, continuous professional development programmes to community educators in 'Transformative Community Education' and 'Technology Enhanced Learning'.

The work of An Cosán VCC is supported by a range of public and private sector partners. IT Carlow supports accredited education provision through An Cosán and VCC, and further supports VCC's engagement with educational technologies. The Department of Social Protection funds key elements of VCC's work. Several corporate sponsors and philanthropists, including the ESB and Three Ireland, provide further financial, technical, and management support. An Cosán VCC, in collaboration with Three Ireland, notably developed an online mentoring system for learners. Crucially, VCC partners with women's groups, family resource, and community education centres around the country to share knowledge and experience and to bring community education, particularly higher education programmes, to communities challenging social inequality.

A key challenge in the development of VCC was to ensure that An Cosán's ethos and philosophy of community education transferred into a blended learning model. To date, this has been achieved through partnering with a growing number of community education centres throughout the island of Ireland. Centres provide facilities where students can access the technology required to engage in blended online learning and create collaborative peer learning communities. They also provide a range of extra-curricular, soft supports for learners to ensure a warm welcome and an encouraging learning atmosphere. These partnerships create invaluable, supportive spaces for students while also making a range of e-learning tools and resources available to community education organisations. In the future, as knowledge and skills develop, these community partnerships will allow quality programmes and best practice emerging at a local level to be mainstreamed nationally.

VCC's 'blended learning' model centres on the development of a collaborative learning community. Every programme begins with a face to face workshop where learners are introduced to tutors, technology moderators, and one another in person. Learners discuss the core pedagogical goals, learning materials, and assessment strategies with the tutor before being introduced to the technology to be used throughout the programme. Technology moderators support learners to engage with the specially designed online learning systems, facilitating their developing digital literacy skills. Depending on the programme, these Virtual Learning Environments operate on Blackboard, Moodle, Office 365 and Adobe Connect. 'Induction Day' is followed by weekly live online sessions using a variety of interactive tools to facilitate group discussion. In VCC's 'flipped classroom', learners access readings, watch videos, and undertake assignments in their own time and at a pace that suits them. A second face-to-face workshop, held mid-way through the programme, gives learners a chance to provide collective feedback on the programme and further develops learners' collaborative relationships. Though still in an early stage of development and growth, initial feedback from community partners and learners concerning VCC's blended learning model is positive and supportive. VCC recently completed a report based on learner evaluations received between January and December, 2016 (VCC 2017). Of the sample of 120 learners, 47% of respondents reported that VCC's blended learning model made it possible for them to participate in higher education. This indicates considerable success in breaking down barriers to lifelong learning. 81% of respondents reported as not having completed education beyond QQI Level 5 (Leaving Certificate), 65% identified issues of confidence in education before enrolling, while 75% specifically identified that they had never taken a course online and felt incapable of using technology for education. By the end of the programme, 65% reported that VCC's courses were successful in improving confidence in their educational ability while 78% indicated that they would recommend their programme to a friend or colleague.

Conclusion

An overriding mantra of the neoliberal austerity agenda is the patently false claim that education is the economic salvation for society, as opposed to state guarantees of full employment, universal health care, affordable housing, low-cost childcare, and other anti-austerity measures that would significantly improve the quality of life for all (Ryan 2016:153). By itself, education cannot eradicate the poverty, unemployment, class oppression, gender inequality, and racism that broadly determine student outcomes and opportunities. This is the reality within which those seeking to address educational inequality are positioned. The expansion of higher education in Ireland has not significantly reduced glaring inequalities of access, notably among poorer socio-economic groups and mature students. Educational equality remains a significant challenge in a society where 99% of students from Dublin 6 will progress to higher education compared to 15% in Dublin 15. Barriers to accessing higher education, including financial cost, childcare considerations, geography, public transport availability and lack of institutional access, have heightened because of recent austerity programmes. Even the EU Commission (2017:41) acknowledges that 'fairness and inclusion' remain a concern in Irish higher education provision, and that funding for appropriate strategies may yet prove 'insufficient'.

At the same time, issues of educational equality must be considered alongside the growing importance of information and communication technologies and of Ireland's digital divide. A wave of digital disruption is rapidly reshaping society and education. The possibilities for connection and learning afforded by today's interconnected world are far greater than those imagined by even the most perspicacious science fiction writers of generations past. In recent years, there has been a significant integration of emergent technologies and teaching and learning strategies into higher education institutions. Here too, however, resources remain lacking. Key challenges remain to provide infrastructure to take advantage of low-cost connectivity and digital storage, to scale educational technologies, and to improve digital literacy (NMC 2015). The condition of Ireland's broadband infrastructure presents a further, related challenge. State investment is undoubtedly required to close the gap in high speed broadband coverage between rural and urban areas (Department of Communications, Energy and Natural Resources 2015). Notwithstanding these adverse circumstances, proponents of imaginative forms of social innovation can help to alleviate embedded educational disadvantages.

An Cosán Virtual Community College is one such initiative, utilising a blended learning model to provide a wide variety of introductory and higher education programmes to learners and communities throughout the island of Ireland. An Cosán VCC's early success demonstrates the potential of 21st century learning technologies to make education accessible. Throughout this assessment, our approach has been neither to deify nor demonise new educational technologies but to consider them from 'a critically curious standpoint' (See Freire 2001:38). Clearly, much depends on the purposes to which these tools are put. A recurring tension between functionalist and emancipatory forms of learning persists within all levels of Ireland's education system. At present, austerity cuts and labour market activation policies risk marginalising much that is emancipatory within community education practice. In sum, as we stated at the outset, the key technical and political challenge for those attempting socially innovative forms of education remains that of combining technology with human empathy in such a way that both communities and individual learners can flourish and fulfil their potential. A new social enterprise drawing on a rich tradition, An Cosán Virtual Community College has attempted to do just that, taking small but significant steps towards addressing educational inequality and demolishing the digital divide in 21st century Ireland. Our journey continues.

CHAPTER 11
REFLECTIONS ON A SOCIAL INNOVATION IN SCHOOL AGE CHILDCARE

Michelle O'Sullivan

Introduction

A dominant paradigm in Ireland's national development in 2002 was the concept of social partnership. Rory O'Donnell, an economist with the National Economic and Social Council (NESC) has written extensively on social partnership and prepared analyses underpinning Ireland's partnership approach to economic and social policy. He advised that social partnership would only remain successful into the future if it could anticipate and help to solve the problems caused by change "Yet partnership only has a future if it continues to be consistent with the dynamic of the economy and society, and if it can anticipate and help to solve the problems which change throws up" (O'Donnell 2001:13).

According to O'Donnell (2001:28) a dilemma for public policy and social partnership, in the context of rapid change, was that neither could address critical structural and supply-side challenges. This includes policies relating to education and childcare, with O'Donnell suggesting that the relevant policies could only be agreed, analysed and changed in the context of doing them. O'Donnell (2000:210) refers to Rorty's (1996:71) suggestion that "the pressure to rise to a higher level of abstraction in philosophy and politics' should come from below and that 'locally useful abstractions should emerge out of local and banal deliberations".

Given the emphasis on partnership (social partnership and partnership in education) and the apparent shortage of school age childcare in Ireland, a local school age childcare initiative offered an opportunity for research which led to a doctoral thesis involving a longitudinal action research case study, which is the basis for this chapter. It documents the progress of a social innovation over a period of 10 years. As an 'intervention and reflective experiment' (Argyris *et al.* 1985) or as an 'interventionist experiment' (Argyris and Schön 1989:613) it sheds light on the every-day, tacit interactions and 'local and

147

banal deliberations' (Rorty 1996:71) of local actors in a primary school in South Dublin as they set about developing a social enterprise in school age childcare.

This chapter reflects on how the school partners embarked on an agenda of social innovation and change to solve local problems. Section 2 briefly outlines the national childcare context when the local innovation was first proposed in 2002. Section 3 describes the local context, the impetus for, and evolution of the social innovation in school age childcare . The fourth section describes the pilot and draws come conclusions as to the relevance of this initiative in the broader childcare context in Ireland. The fifth section concludes the chapter.

The National Context

Prior to the 1990s Ireland experienced a vicious circle of extensive and persistent emigration (Mjoset 1992). However, a decade after Mjoset's analysis the situation in Ireland had changed dramatically. Unemployment stood at 4.2% in 2002 (Government of Ireland 2003) compared to 17% in 1987 (Boyd 2002). Peadar Kirby (2002:64) notes that "one positive social impact of the Celtic Tiger has been the substantial increase in women's participation in the labour force". Fahey, Russell and Smyth (2000) indicate an increase from 28% in 1971 to 44% in 1999. While this was still low compared to European standards of female labour force participation, Kirby (2002) notes Ireland's movement towards convergence with the European average during the 1990s.

However, these positive statistics hide a variation in levels of participation, as indicated by Fahey *et al.* (2000) in their work on gender equality, fertility and work patterns for Irish women. They found that Ireland's labour force participation rates among women with children under five years of age were the lowest in Europe at the end of the 1990s, with rates among women with children under ten years of age faring only slightly better (Ibid). Access to childcare and patterns of participation in the labour force are gender-related. The local context for this case study supports Fahey *et al.*'s (2000) contention, and indicates that a lack of accessibility to school age childcare is an obstacle for the continuing labour force participation of mothers.

By 2002, the booming Celtic Tiger economy was dependent on an expansion of the labour force, with women's increasing participation in paid employment seen as one of the means to achieve this. In this context, childcare was not just a major issue for women with young children, but also an important issue for national policy and the social partners.

Policy development in school age childcare has been a challenge in Ireland. A concerted approach to this sector has proven elusive over the past three decades. While interest in childcare has intensified since the 1980s, (with women's groups and trade unions taking the lead and a number of policy reports emerging) until the 1990s any development in childcare services in Ireland was mainly due to the voluntary sector (Hayes 2006), and predominantly focused on pre-school age childcare.

An EC report emphasised very low state support for childcare in Ireland compared to all other European countries (European Commission Childcare Network 1990). This finding increased demand on the government to support and develop the childcare sector (Hayes 2002). From the mid-1990s, Ireland's rapidly growing economic prosperity led to a shortage of workers, and the social partners added their voices to the demand for childcare (Hayes 2002). The Partnership 2000 negotiations in 1996 combined the influence of the unions, business and the community pillar on the policy implications of a robust Early Childhood Care and Education (ECCE) sector, and childcare issues rose to the top of the national policy agenda (Hayes 2002). In 1997, a working group, known as the P2000 Expert Working Group on Childcare ('the Expert Group'), was set-up by the Department of Justice, Equality and Law Reform to develop an integrated strategy for ECCE services. The Expert Group was also mandated to consider school age childcare services. As a result this was the first time that the sector had been included on the policy agenda (Hayes 2002).

Funding Childcare in Ireland
The Equal Opportunities Childcare Programme (EOCP1) was introduced in 1998 with £11m of EU and £14m of exchequer funding. This was an important step towards government incentives for childcare services (Hayes 2006). Funding for childcare services was originally increased to €317.4m under the

National Development Plan (NDP) during the period 2000–2006 (Hayes 2006). Although funding for school age childcare was not included in this. The Cabinet Sub-Committee on Social Inclusion subsequently reviewed funding for school age childcare and responsibility for this was assigned to the Department of Justice, Equality and Law Reform in March 2001. Subsequent to this review, EOCP funding was increased to €453m, part-funded by the exchequer and part-funded from the European Regional Development Fund (ERDF): €154m for capital funding, €202m for staffing funding, and €87m for the Quality Initiative, with the remaining €10m funding unspecified (Hayes 2006).

The report 'Developing Childcare in Ireland' (Department of Justice Equality and Law Reform 2004) refers to €9m allocated to the EOCP, some for school age childcare, which had received exchequer funding only, and some for the Quality Sub-Measure at the Spring 2004 monitoring committees. In comparison to the level of funding in other areas of childcare, a portion of €9m for school age childcare was a very minor sum, and this lack of funding, combined with an almost complete absence of any policy development, partly explains the under-provision of formal school age childcare.

Affordability of Childcare (for parents)
John Bennett, co-author of two volumes of *Starting Strong*, the first with Michelle Neuman (OECD 2001) and the second with Collette Taylor (OECD 2006), has been involved with the OECD Early Childhood Reviews since 1998. He argues that Ireland is a classical liberal economy, typified by low government spending, and noticeable poverty at the base of society. In terms of relative affordability he cites childcare costs in Ireland as accounting for approximately 30% of disposable family income compared to an EU average of 8% (Bennett 2006).

Another outcome of under funding is an inequitable childcare market which modest-income families in the third and fourth quintiles find hard to access. As a result it makes little economic sense for many mothers to return to work when a second child is born (Bennett 2006). This is supported by local experience prior to 2002, which also indicates that the problem is more critical when a first child starts school rather than when they are born, due to a lack of school age childcare facilities locally. This suggests that there might be a latent demand for school age childcare places if the issues of affordability and availability are not addressed through policy initiatives[53].

Conceptions of Childhood Institutions

Dahlberg, Moss and Pence (1999) outline four conceptualisations of early childhood institutions: (1) as services; (2) as a means of social intervention; (3) as pursuing educational tasks; and 4) as forums in civil society that serve their local communities. An analysis of Ireland's policy approach to childcare includes promoting it as a service for working parents and as a social intervention to target disadvantage and inequality. Other policy objectives in early childhood care and education include preparing children for compulsory school, particularly in the context of children living in disadvantaged areas (this doubles up as a social intervention). There has also been a tradition in Ireland of early childhood services preparing children for compulsory (primary) school, with private providers catering for middle class families, and, more recently, through government supports for families in disadvantaged areas. This equates to the first three of Dahlberg *et al.*'s (1999) four conceptualisations of early childhood institutions. In each of these areas it could be argued that the underlying rationale is economic, and to improve chances for economic success.

Impetus for Social Innovation in School Age Childcare

In a sense, the first three conceptualisations of early childhood institutions reflect an unquestioning acceptance of norms suggested in the work of Chomsky (2004). The case study suggests that schools, families and communities tacitly prefer the fourth option proposed by Dahlberg *et al* (1999), which advocates that childhood institutions be conceptualised as forums in civil society that are inclusive of local communities, similar to Moss's (2001) concept of childcare institutions as sites

---

[53] While there have been some moves in tackling issues of access and affordability since 2014, availability of school age childcare places remains an issue. The very recent *Action Plan for School Age Childcare* jointly published by the Departments of Children and Youth Affairs, and Education and Skills in March 2017, provides a comprehensive review of school age childcare, together with an action plan for policy development in this area.

of democratic experimentalism. However, the mainstream options available in Ireland in 2002 were those catered for in national policy and in current childcare practice. These were predominantly focused on the pre-school age childcare sector, and fell into one of the first three approaches to childhood institutions proposed by Dahlberg *et al.* (1999).

The Local Context

This case study is situated in a primary school located in Dublin, a Catholic but not a parish school established in 1963 as a fee-paying school (Heffernan 2007). Subsequently, the school joined the Department of Education free education scheme for primary schools in 1971. The original school building, built by the Trustees in the early 1960s, was comprised of four classrooms and a school hall. This was expanded over the years as pupil numbers increased and prefabs for nine additional classes were added between the main school building and the school yard. By 2002 several of the prefabs, which had been in situ for over 30 years, were in poor condition.

The Trustees had applied to the Department of Education for a new school in the late 1980s to cater for the rapid growth in pupil numbers. It wasn't until 1998 that the Department (now renamed as the Department of Education and Skills) agreed in principal that a new school would be included in the schools building list[54]. Following this announcement fundraising was undertaken by the parents' council to build up the local funds for this new school building.

During the three years prior to this study (1999–2002) pupil numbers in the school had substantially declined (from almost 380 to just under 280). In November 2001 a questionnaire was sent to parents from the board of management to assess their attitudes to different aspects of the school and curriculum. The feedback was very positive but provided little indication of the reasoning for the fall in pupil numbers.

By 2002 some key initiatives had emerged from discussions among the school partners which offered mutual benefits for the school, families and children in order to address falling pupil numbers. The first initiative involved a change in school status

---

[54] The new school building wasn't completed until 2012.

from 'girls only' to 'co-educational'. It had been noted at parents' council meetings during 2001 that some of the local boys' schools had changed their enrolment policies to take boys in from junior infants. As a result, many families were moving their boys out of the school prior to the forecasted move at the end of second class. The board of management survey found that most respondent parents were in favour of this. By June 2002 an agreement was reached with all the relevant parties, including the Department of Education and Skills (DES), to change the school's status.

The second initiative, which was never formally progressed, was inspired by the recently introduced Education Act and its provisions relating to the inclusion of parents as partners in school policy and planning. The intention was to develop a school plan showing how supports for the school might be prioritised when funds from the childcare service became available.

Local experience indicated that access to school age childcare was an issue which meant mothers were were unable to plan for their return to paid employment. In 2002 a group of parents decided to address the shortage of access to local school age childcare. This led to the third initiative; a proposal for a school age childcare service to be run by parents as part of the school partnership. The intention was that this could help to reverse the fall in pupil numbers, as well as contributing resources to the school over time. This chapter follows the early stages of this initiative and focuses on the circumstances leading to the social innovation in school age childcare instigated by the school partners.

The idea of a school age childcare service originally began as a joke during conversations with three other mothers in late 2000. Each of us had two or more children, and all of us had stopped working when the eldest child started primary school due to a lack of local school age childcare. All of us were volunteers on the Parents' Council at the time. With the announcement of childcare grants in the 2001 Budget we decided to raise the issue at the parents' council meeting in January 2001.

Parents' Council Discussions - Towards a Family Focus
The change in school status and an after-school childcare service were viewed as family-focused initiatives. Both would make life easier for families, and perhaps create a greater sense of community. Thus, the childcare concept emerged not only as a means of counteracting the decline in enrolments, but also to address a shortage in school age childcare which was a real concern for working parents. By late 2001 the parents' council agreed that there was merit in the concept and asked me to prepare a formal written proposal.

Initial Proposal
The main elements of the childcare proposal were that the service would be set up as a co-operative under the management of the parents' council, on the assumption that this would qualify for charity status. There would be a paid business manager to oversee operations, and care would be provided by 20–25 volunteers, each contributing four to five hours per week, for which they would receive time-in-lieu. Those using the service but not volunteering would pay a fee and profits would be managed by the parents' council for three purposes: improvements in the childcare service; upgrading school equipment (which could also be used by the childcare service); and contribution towards school running costs. The board of management responded positively to the proposal, or at least there was a 'provisional consensus to proceed with practical action' (O'Donnell 1998:103).

Local Research - Parental Interest in Participation
During the first half of 2002 a survey was conducted to garner the levels of interest among parents to participate in the setting up of this initiative. There were 131 respondents to this survey (response rate of 47%, split between 78 mothers and 53 fathers). The types of participation parents were interested in is indicated in the following table;

154

Table 11.1: Types of Participation

	% Responses	
Statement	Yes	No
Willing to participate in setting up a childcare service	23	77
Willing to participate in computer training for parents	38	62
Willing to participate in workshops for school policy and planning	37	63
Willing to participate in learning about educational issues	54	46
Willing to participate in parenting classes	43	57
Source: O'Sullivan (2002:69 Table 5.13).		

This indicates that there a higher response among parents in 'learning about educational issues' and 'willing to participate in learning about educational issues', and 'participation in parenting classes' than either participating in 'workshops for school policy and planning' or 'setting up a childcare service'. Less than a quarter of respondents indicated a willingness to participate in setting up a childcare service, which raised doubts about the potential feasibility of progressing with the childcare proposal.

A survey conducted in the school (O'Sullivan 2002) included questions on parents' work patterns to determine if there was any difference in attitudes to school partnership among mothers and fathers, and between parents who were in paid employment or not.

An analysis is contained within Table 11.2. The local survey appears to indicate a higher female participation rate in 2002 than the 44% suggested by Fahy et al. (1999). This could be influenced by at least three factors: first, it could reflect the trend of increasing labour force participation among mothers since 1999; second, it might represent socio-economic factors where there are more dual income households in the local context than the national picture indicates; and third, it doesn't include women in older age categories where labour force participation tends to be lower.

The local survey involved a very small sample of parents in one location, and, while it cannot claim to be representative, it provides some insight into working patterns among mothers with school age children that aren't apparent in national labour force statistics. A closer look at the statistics in the local survey indicates that almost half of mothers were in paid part-time employment, while almost a third were involved in unpaid home duties.

Table 11.2: Gender and Occupation of Respondents

Employment Category	Fathers	Mothers
Full-time paid employment, away from home	88.7%	14.1%
Part-time employment, away from home	3.8%	46.2%
Full- or part-time employment, in the home	3.8%	6.4%
Unpaid employment, in the home.	3.8%	33.3%
Source: Adapted from (O'Sullivan 2002:58 Table 5.3)		

Breaking this down 14% of mothers surveyed were in full-time employment outside the home, 46% were working part-time hours, and 6% were working from home. This suggests that most mothers in paid employment adopt working patterns that are flexible. There is also an indication of strong gender differentials in paid employment and unpaid home duties between mothers and fathers with children of primary school age in this school.

Feasibility

Therefore, while there were indications that the school age childcare initiative was a worthwhile idea, by the end of June, 2002 it was difficult to see how it might progress, or indeed whether it was feasible at all. However, unwilling to give up on the idea, I pondered its value and feasibility with others over Summer 2002. I discussed it with the principal, who encouraged me to push ahead, suggesting that I get a team of volunteer parents on board. I contacted respondents to the questionnaire who had indicated an interest in helping to set up a childcare service. By the start of September, I had gathered a group of seven mothers who were willing to commit to volunteer their time to mind children. We drew up a rota between us to provide cover for two hours per day, five days a week for the academic year (September – June).

The school had agreed to lend us a room, tables and chairs and the parents' council provided us with a loan of €600 to cover initial expenses, such as insurance. Therefore, we felt that we had sufficient resources and volunteers on board to at least conduct a pilot to test the concept, which we started in September 2002. A PhD scholarship from DIT in November, 2002, to conduct an action research study on the school age childcare initiative provided another resource.

Financial Considerations
Working on the adage that desperation is the mother of invention, and owing to the fact that financial resources were limited, we decided on some creative ways of managing early finances. To secure some up-front income we decided to implement an initial registration fee of €25 for any family using the service, and to set our rates at €9 per day (for an hour and three-quarters). Thus, the seven volunteers and fee-paying families added €300 to the start-up kitty by way of registration fees, and our initial income was a modest €100 per week. This was enough to repay the parents' council loan, pay for insurance, company set-up fees and other minor expenses, and still have a small surplus (€600) at the end of June 2003. The parents' council had been unable to determine which Government department was dealing with childcare grants when the school age childcare concept was first raised in 2001. In early September 2002, the childcare volunteers decided to look for this information again, and discovered that the grants were the responsibility of the Department of Justice, Equality and Law Reform (DJELR) under the Equal Opportunities Childcare Programme (EOCP), and were administered by Area Development Management Ltd (ADM).

Initially, we decided to apply for staffing grants to fund two part-time employees, one of whom would manage the day-to-day operations. The intention was that this should provide funding for a year at least, which would facilitate longer opening hours after the pilot. Then, in mid-September 2002, the school board of management informed us that they couldn't commit to lending us the prefab for more than one year at a time, as pupil numbers had already increased slightly. They suggested that we seek a site from the trustees on which to locate a more permanent building for the childcare service. The original proposal hadn't considered issues such as a site or the need to approach the trustees in relation to this. We were also unaware at that stage that, while the board of management had authority to sanction our use of the prefab as we were providing a service with educational benefits (i.e. school supports), only the trustees, as owners of the school grounds, had the authority to lease us a site. Nor had we considered the immediate financial implications of having to fund our own premises, and quickly realised that we would also need to apply for capital grants for this.

Volunteers

A related early decision was whether volunteers should receive in-lieu childcare hours. While this had been referred to in the childcare proposal, the number of volunteer hours in-lieu for childcare hadn't been decided. Our consensus was that it was a good idea and might encourage others to volunteer. We agreed on two hours of childcare in lieu of every volunteer hour worked.[55] Time spent on administration, operations, grant application and planning meetings didn't receive time-in-lieu as we felt that this time might be difficult to quantify (however, it was more difficult to get volunteers actively involved in these aspects).

Challenges and Learnings

In this section I reflect on the challenges posed to the childcare volunteers and school partners in developing a community based childcare initiative, and the learnings that can be taken from this experience in a broader context.

Under-Provision of School Age Childcare

Soon after commencing the pilot, and once we had gathered information on what was required for the grant applications, the childcare volunteers realized that the notion of operating as a co-operative under the auspices of the parents' council was

---

[55] This was reduced to one hour the following year.

158

insufficient as an organizational structure. However, we found it difficult to find appropriate examples of how different models of school age childcare operated in Ireland and looked to examples we had discovered abroad. A review of the literature in 2002 and 2003 indicated that policy attention to the school age sector barely existed. This correlated with our local findings. It seemed a bit odd to us that policy makers would fail to recognize that if parents required childcare for younger children, they might continue to need care when those children started going to school, and that this was likely to occur within a four-year cycle.

We found a predominant focus in Ireland on the pre-school age sector, and scarcity of school age childcare provision. This was supported by an evaluation of childcare services across the EU (European Commission Childcare Network 1990). This stated that Ireland was among three countries with little sign of any significant development of formal school age childcare (Meijvogel and Petrie 1996). In contrast, the pre-school sector had developed significantly since the 1980s, and particularly since the 1990s, when a formal childcare – or, more accurately, pre-school sector emerged in Ireland.

Assessing Models from Abroad
We reviewed other international models of school age childcare. We discarded the French model as it was fully state supported and not a runner given childcare policy in Ireland. We discussed the Norwegian model, which was state supported and subsidised with parents paying according to what they could afford (this was managed by an external agency). While we felt this might provide an equitable scheme for families and children, it was not an option, as again it was not part of the policy environment in Ireland. One of the volunteer's experience of school age childcare in Canada provided us with some new ideas. Here, parents using the service were obliged to contribute to their share of childcare. We discarded this option for several reasons; the potential difficulty of getting sufficient parents to volunteer, that those parents might not be interested or trained in childcare, that managing a large body of parent volunteers might be too onerous to co-ordinate, and that it might not deliver a service oriented to children's needs.

A Scottish model provided a good example of state funded and supported childcare. We got information on a local after school care facility that had been set up and established by a group of volunteer parents in Ayr, Scotland. Here, a separate paid management company was contracted to carry out the routine management and operational aspects of the service. Funding was received from state bodies to provide low-cost, quality childcare, with parents paying some fees, and a voluntary management committee was responsible for monitoring and control of the service. We felt this model might provide us with an adequate template to work on and this, together with some Irish pre-school examples we had collected, gave us sufficient information to proceed.

The next phase of co-ordination therefore involved attempting to secure a site and grant funding. These aspects provided catalysts for action and reflection on a range of activities that helped to refine our community and not-for-profit aspirations and model of school age childcare.

Policies and Procedures for School Age Childcare

We were unable to find policies and procedures for Irish school age childcare, so we collected examples from services providing pre-school age childcare. During the pilot we also discovered that there are many differences between the school age and the pre-school sectors, as the following examples indicate.

When deliberating on the grant application process the childcare volunteers were often confused over what constituted 'school age' and 'pre-school age' childcare. Our interpretation of the age band that our service should cater for was four to 12 years: the age range of children attending the school. Attendance at full-time education is not compulsory before six years of age, although most children start formal education in their fifth or sixth year, and most four- to six-year-olds are enrolled in the infant classes in primary schools (Department of Education and Science 2001). Early Childhood Care and Education (ECCE) provision refers to the zero to six years age cohort and the childcare regulations are for this age group, but, as we discovered, there was no regulatory environment governing school age childcare, or indeed for four- to six-year-olds in primary schools who are attending childcare services outside school hours. In the absence of regulatory guide-lines we agreed to adopt the recommended ratios for children in the four+ age range.

In our discussions as to why there was a discrepancy in the regulatory treatment of pre-school and school-going children, we came to the tentative conclusion that if regulations were put in place for school age childcare this would open a can of worms for the DES in that schools had up to 30 (and often more) children in classes with one teacher; the space allocated to each child was considerably less than that required by the pre-school regulations; and the structural constraints in schools meant that they wouldn't be able to adhere to the same requirements for food and health and safety. Regulating school age childcare might set the benchmark for schools, with financial implications for the DES and potentially pitting one government department's vested interest against another's (e.g. Education and Skills versus Justice and Equality).

Conclusion
The case study is an action research project using a bottom-up, non-traditional research approach, in line with what Urban (2006) advocates in the New Zealand model. This research, and the experience of local participants, has tapped into a clear preference by parents for care and education that is integrated and inclusive of the community (including the school), working with and drawing on it, to provide the best learning and caring outcomes for children.

In Ireland, little explicit attention has been given to the role childhood institutions (including primary schools, school partnerships, and childcare services) can play in serving local communities as forums in civil society, apart perhaps from such services as parents' and toddlers' groups, or to some degree with the development of social capital in community-based childcare services in disadvantaged areas. This perhaps represents a missed opportunity in bringing viable alternatives to current discussions and debates on school age childcare provision in Ireland. The current action research study suggests that primary school partnerships represent forums in civil society (Dahlberg *et al.* 1999), where if encouraged, democratic experimentalism and social innovation can evolve to address local needs.

SECTION IV
WAY FORWARD

CHAPTER 12
SOCIAL INNOVATION: LEARNINGS AND PERSPECTIVES

Jordana Corrigan

Introduction

The contributions in this volume by practitioners and academics allow us to reflect on the varying perspectives and ideal conditions for social innovation across multiple sectors. The 'wicked problems' as described by the contributors prevail; – hunger, financial inequality, poverty, social welfare. New challenges are also emerging in contemporary society; climate change, globalisation, an ageing population, migration and urbanization. Ireland is still recovering from the financial crises and there is arguably, in political discussions at least, an overwhelming and narrow measurement of everything in economic terms with a rhetoric of 'value to the economy' and 'economic growth'[56].

There is consensus amongst the contributors that the language and definitions of 'social innovation', social enterprise' and 'social entrepreneurship' are varied. Perhaps at the root of this problem is the absence of any clear cross-sectoral policy guidance in Ireland. The absence of such policy guidance constrains the development of a favourable ecosystem for social innovation. As discussed by Munck and Ó Broin, divorcing politics from the discussion on social innovation and the social economy can be misleading or unhelpful.

The contributions highlight for discussion the need for us to be explicit and questioning in our motivations and means for improving society. The views from practitioners and academics alike suggest that risk aversion and bureaucracy has slowed progress in the past and that we need to be more agile in our processes and administration. It is also apparent that we need to be clearer as to how we measure social innovation. There is a lack of robust quantitative and qualitative data on the impact of social innovation is understandable given that the measurement

---

[56] For further discussion see The Econocracy (Earle *et al* 2016) and Doughnut Economics (Raworth 2017).

of it is a complex process requiring further academic and practitioner research I would argue.

Definitions

There is a general consensus evident in the contributions that Ireland needs a national strategy on social innovation and that a favourable ecosystem for social innovation is dependent upon both civil society and government support. The origins and development of social innovation on the island of Ireland are described as being manifested in community development and charitable work, cooperatives, philanthropic efforts, and state supports in the form of policies and financing to tackle embedded social problems. Ó Broin and Munck have addressed the role of politics in the discussion on social innovation. Mortell and Garvey have described and discussed the role of the state in funding social innovation in the Irish context. The contributions on the sectors of education, justice, childcare and healthcare have offered specific examples of how state policies and departments have impacted, with various degrees of success, upon social innovation in these sectors.

Social innovation is subject to many definitions. Mulgan *et al.* (2007:8) state that they prefer the simple one which is "new ideas that work". The key question when using this simple definition is what we mean by the word 'work'. New technologies offer many opportunities to contribute towards solving our societal problems through better management and sharing of resources, more efficient logistics and increased collaboration and networking. In that sense they 'work'. They are relatively cheap to develop, maintain and easily replicable. New technologies in social innovation cannot be limited to increasing efficiencies, they must also be disruptive to prompt social change. The potential for using digital technology as a means for engaging the key stakeholders in the innovation process can't be ignored. However, these types of solutions may lack inclusivity as not everyone feels able to engage with these on-line platforms. Further, valuable 'civic rewards' lie in the engagement, interaction and knowledge transfer of interpersonal relationships (Russon Gilman 2016). Technological innovations in the form of services and products do not create impact if these outcomes do not progress to engage and reach the people that need them (Seelos and Mair, 2016:5).

What we might understand as scaling up of innovation is therefore extremely important. We must be clear as to what we mean by scaling up i.e. is it replicating a service or product that has 'worked' in one context into another. Or is it about ensuring that the innovation results in an outcome for society that has ultimately improved the traditional way of doing things, increasing participation and deepening democracy. Participatory budgeting is perhaps a good example in this regard as it is an accepted and proven social innovation, but it is highly context - specific, the success of which depends on the ability of those involved to reflect on, and adapt the process to their unique contexts (Russon Gilman 2016). Peer lending which matches potential investors with borrowers via online platforms has also seen very different levels of success in Bangladesh and the US due to the widely varied operating conditions (Dees *et al.* 2002).

Nesta (2014) published a report on the processes for scaling up social innovation. It builds on the work by Dees *et al.* (2002) who write about a matrix view of scaling up for social entrepreneurs. It asks two questions; what do we scale? How do we do it? They describe a framework where the 'what' is typically categorised as a program, organisation or set of principles. Using the example of a learning centre that has been particularly effective in teaching maths to pre-school children, Dees (2002) describes how this particular innovation could be defined and replicated successfully in three different ways; (a) as a programme i.e. a math curriculum for use in day care centres (b) as an organisational model (if the success was down to a distinctive organisational environment) and (c) as a core set of principles about how teachers, students, and parents interact.

The 'how' categorises the mechanisms to use to scale the process eg (a) "dissemination" describes the sharing of information with the originating organization providing some form of technical assistance as to how the innovation can be adapted for a different context (b) "affiliation" describes an ongoing agreement between two or more parties to be part of a network and (c) "branching" occurs when the bodies implementing the innovation are legally part of one large organization (Ibid).

The Nesta (2014:14) report provides more prescriptive advice on the routes to scaling up innovation, and multiple case studies. The report again highlights the importance that "social innovators need to be clear on their goals for the type and scale of social impact they want to achieve". Being clear on the goal will determine the 'what' and 'how' of what is right to scale (Nesta 2014, Dees *et al.* 2002). Dee's (2002) matrix framework is particularly useful as it very simply and effectively provides the space to think about scaling up innovations by packaging them for different contexts in different ways through existing and new organisations, or a combination of both. It also raises the question of 'who' scales innovation. In some cases we may not be best placed to scale the innovation and the most valuable work that we can do is to find the resources or to make the connections with partnerships that can. Nesta (2014:14) also make the point that when scaling up "it's also good to be aware of more personal goals, preferences and needs. These include values, personal aspirations as a leader and financial considerations". I think that these factors contribute towards risk aversion and and behaviour change in a broader sense and these are addressed in the section which follows.

Risk
The element of risk is described as being a significant limiting factor in the discussion of social innovation. The level of risk; risk of failure, risk of making the wrong decision, risk of supporting an unpopular initiative are very difficult to measure and perhaps hide the real and inherent risk that we are naturally resistant to behavior change.

Mulgan *et al.* (2007:18) outlines that for innovators the barriers to change "often look like personal failings on the part of the powerful: their stupidity, rigidity and lack of imagination is all that stands between a brilliant new idea and its execution. But the barriers to change go much deeper than this". We need to understand the root causes of resistance to behavioral change and that regard I think we can start with Mulgan's summary and think in terms of efficiency, interests, minds and relationships.

People might resist the most reasonable reforms because in the short term they threaten efficiency and performance. "Even public sectors which by many standards are highly inefficient will have built up their own logic (Ibid:18). In order to change behavior, organisations must do two things; cultivate the potentially higher impact innovation acknowledging that it may fail, and "ride both the old and the new waves – how, in some cases, to compete against yourself" (Ibid:18).

The second barrier to change as described by Mulgan *et al.* (2007) relates to people's interests – "the risk of change will appear great compared to the benefits of continuity" (Ibid:18). People are reluctant to discard past practices that they have invested time and money in, particularly if the current system if working to their own ends.

The third barrier is 'minds', meaning the values, assumptions and norms that are embedded in the social system. A system that appears to work the more it becomes entrenched and organisations then become locked into routines and habits that are "as much psychological as practical" (Ibid:18).

The final barrier would be in regards to the personal relationships between the stakeholders in the system. Social capital is a stabilizing factor and while the "networks of favours and debts can be key for getting things to happen within a stable system, but they are likely to seriously impede any radical change" (Ibid:18).

The changes that need to be made as we move forward with the social innovation agenda, as outlined in the previous chapters, require some very open and honest discussions. Perhaps the four barriers as suggested by Mulgan *et al.* (2007) provide a good reference point to tease out and discuss the issues of risk i.e. where exactly does the risk lie, is it about:

- Temporarily reducing effectiveness to trial something (that may fail) in the interests of improving impact?
- Losing the practices that we have invested time and money in that work for us?
- Changing our routines and habits which may be as much psychological as practical?
- Changing our network which gets things done, but is not likely to yield any radical change?

These questions are also relevant in the conversation on measurement of social innovation which is discussed further in the following section. The Bureau of European Policy Advisers

(BEPA) (2014:22) describe how measuring social innovation is difficult as success relies on factors which are difficult to quantify and relies on "how they have been able to act as drivers of social change, to break with established approaches and to engage a process of changing behaviours, 'basic routines, resource and authority flows, or beliefs of the social system' in which they occur".

Working towards cross border social innovation is arguably highly risky if we consider it in terms of the issues above not least because of the levels of behavioural change required to work across jurisdictions. However, we could argue that it is both practical and necessary in the context of an impending Brexit and that the potential rewards are also very significant.

Research and Measurement

Mulgan *et al.* (2007:5) argue that "the lack of knowledge impedes the many institutions interested in this field, including innovators themselves, philanthropists, foundations and governments, and means that far too many rely on anecdotes and hunches". Mortell supports this argument in an Irish context describing a lack of quantitative data and case studies as posing a challenge to the translation of what we mean by social innovation into policy, and that we need increased academic and practitioner research in this regard.

In the discussion on ecosystems in the previous section we have seen a favourable ecosystem for social innovation in terms of our history of tackling social problems, society and financing. However, we lack the space to "develop methodologies from empirical and theoretical observations to develop or scale up successful experiments. Thus, research is an essential component of the ecosystem" (BEPA 2014:22). Through research we can create

> catalysing places and instruments where collective work is valued and recognised (or at least not penalised). Incubators to generate the birth and growth as well as tools to exchange, compare and value are other essential components of the social innovation ecosystem (Ibid).

BEPA (2014:22) identify four reasons for addressing the challenge of measuring social innovation which are summarised as (1) need to prove that social innovation is actually an effective and sustainable way to address social needs (2) need to justify the spending of public and private financing (3) evidence based polices require predictions of the expected impact (4) innovations could allow European economies to develop a competitive advantage showing that "social and environmental value creation is central to the human and ecological sustainability of societies".

The measurement of social innovation is complex. The Economist Intelligence Unit has recently published The Social Innovation Index 2016 which measures the capacity for social innovation across the G20, OECD nations, and some select countries to illustrate some notable trends in developing economies. Each country has been scored across four pillars that are considered to 'underpin' their capacity to develop social innovation; institutional framework, financing, entrepreneurship, and society.

Ireland ranks 19th overall in the study with a score of 56.5, the highest ranking country is the US (79.4), followed by the UK (77.3), the Philippines are the lowest ranking at 27.6. Unsurprisingly, in the context of the contributions in this volume Ireland's lowest score is in the area of policy and institutional framework ranking 33rd out of 45 with a score of 33.8. By comparison the UK leads the ranking in this category at 86.6. Ireland's highest ranking (3rd) with a score of 83.7 is in the area of 'society', after Iceland (88.3) and Denmark (83.9) and ahead of the UK which ranks 14th (64.9). While the UK is ranked 5th in financing (65.1) and entrepreneurship (68.4) by comparison to Ireland which ranks 6th and 10th respectively.

It is important to note that the 'policy and institutional framework' category is the most heavily weighted (44.4%) of the four categories. The justification for this, as documented in the study, is that a stable environment and government commitment is of great importance in enabling social innovation. This reinforces the earlier contention that divorcing politics from the discussion is futile.

The 'financing' category is allocated 22.2% of the index, followed by society (18.3%) and entrepreneurship (15%). It is encouraging that the UK and Ireland both rank highly in the financing category which assesses the availability of financing to support the growth of social enterprises, social entrepreneurs and other socially innovative businesses. What is interesting in the context of all-island social innovation is the divergence between the areas of policy and institutional framework, and society between the two jurisdictions. The society category measures the strength of civil society and values that indicate cultural norms such as volunteerism and trust. I refer to this study for the purposes of demonstrating the multi-faceted approach to measuring social innovation. It also poses some interesting questions as to how we can, on an all-island basis, leverage and learn from each jurisdiction's strengths across the different facets of measurement in moving forward with an all-island social innovation agenda.

Moving Forward
BEPA (2014:55) describes how the awareness of social innovation has grown but while policies have begun to foster social innovation, we are not even half way to the benefits that can be achieved. We need to "move beyond the expanding myriad of small initiatives and projects with limited results – as successful as they are – to achieve a real systemic change that puts social innovation at the heart of all processes and policies". The report outlines three categories for doing so; improve governance in relation to social innovation, focus on knowledge and support, encourage and improve the business environment.

Firstly, improving governance is described as requiring more permanent support for the role of the public sector in innovation and social innovation by "fostering the link between social innovation and the private sector, in particular by improving framework conditions to enable the development of enduring partnerships; making corporate social responsibility a systematic and essential element of analysis and operating mode of all businesses" (BEPA 2014:55). Secondly, it is recommended that we improve our knowledge in the areas of impact measurement and mapping so that we can test new models and focus on best practices or favour bottom-up approaches while also developing our understanding as to how ICT can be incorporated into social innovation. Finally, the BEPA (2014:56) report states that we should support, encourage and improve the business environment specifically with regard to "accessing finance; encouraging partnerships to support social innovation; using public procurements as a genuine social policy instrument; and developing a second phase of the Social Business Initiative".

The goal of these recommendations is ultimately to develop policies which address the ongoing struggle against inequality, to bring about a different conception of the economy that is not focused solely on growth, and to empower citizens (BEPA 2014). In this regard Mulgan *et al.* (2007) describe a 'connected difference' theory of social innovation which emphasises three key dimensions of most important social innovations. They are described as 1. being a combination of existing elements rather than wholly new, 2. they require cross-cutting efforts across organisations, sectors and disciplines and 3. they result in new social relationships. Cross border collaboration is clearly a major and complex social innovation which would have a significant impact. A North South Social Innovation Network could provide the framework for encouraging cross border collaboration and can drive the social innovation agenda on a cross border basis. It might also be the 'catalyst' for driving cross-sectoral multi-stakeholder research and measurement of social innovation, blending academic research with practical theory, benefiting society across jurisdictions.

APPENDICES

APPENDIX 1
Table of Grantees of Social Innovation Fund Ireland 2015-17 (31 grantees totalling 32 grants)
*NFS – value of non-financial supports provided

Animate 2016 (4)

Project Name	Issue focus	Target Group	Location	Impact	Grant size €
ReCreate	Environment / education	Learners of all age/ability	Dublin	Dublin	€20,000 (€10,000 cash, €10,000 NFS*)
Save a Selfie	Physical health	People experiencing cardiac arrest	Meath	Nationwide	€20,000 (€10,000 cash, €10,000 NFS*)
Thriftify	Environment	Charity causes supported by charity shops	Dublin	Nationwide	€20,000 (€10,000 cash, €10,000 NFS*)
CareBright Village	Homecare provision (dementia patients)	People living with dementia and their carers and loved ones	Limerick	Munster region	€20,000 (€20,000 NFS*)

THINKTECH 2016 (4)

Project name	Issue focus	Target Group	Location	Impact	Grant size €
iScoil	Education	Early school leavers or those at risk of leaving school (13-18)	Dublin	Nationwide	€210,000 (€160,000 cash, €50,000 NFS)
Food Cloud Hubs	Food poverty/ food waste	People experiencing food poverty	Dublin	Cork, Dublin & Galway	€220,000 (€170,000 cash, €50,000

					NFS)
The ALONE Platform	Social inclusion/ older people	Older people living alone	Dublin/ Dundalk	Dublin, Louth, Laois & Cork	€220,000 (€170,00 0 cash, €50,000 NFS)
Space Engager s	Homelessness	People experiencin g or at risk of homelessne ss	Dublin	Dublin, Roscommon Kildare, Longford & Clare.	€100,000 (€100,00 0 cash

Engage & Educate 2017 (4)

Project Name	Issue focus	Target Group	Location	Impact	Grant size €
Blossom Gateway	Education/ disability	Teens with intellectual disabilities	Dublin	Dublin	€37,500 (€27,500 cash, €10,000 NFS)
Intercultural Language Service	Social inclusion/ Education	Adult migrants	Dublin	Dublin	€37,500 (€27,500 cash, €10,000 NFS)
Ready Steady Circus	Education/ Life skills	Students in DEIS primary schools	Galway	Galway City & Galway County	€37,500 (€27,500 cash, €10,000 NFS)
Resilience Academy	Educational resilience	Second year students at second level school	Dublin	Dublin, Kildare, Tipperary, Mayo, Galway, Longford, Cork, Limerick, Leitrim & Sligo	€37,500 (€27,500 cash & €10,000 NFS)

Education Fund 2017 (10)

Project Name	Issue focus	Target Group	Location	Impact	Grant size €
An Cosán Virtual Community College	Educational dis- advantage	Adults belonging to groups that are	Dublin	Nationwid e	€452,160

(VCC)		traditionally disenfranchised from higher education			
Aspire 2	Educational dis-advantage	Leaving Certificate students	Dublin and Cork	Dublin and Cork	€370,520
Churchfield Community Trust	Educational dis-advantage	Adults who are at risk or who have a criminal record	Cork	Cork	€70,650
Cork Life Centre	Educational dis-advantage	Young people who have had to leave school for various reasons	Cork	Cork	€314,000
Fast Track Academy "City Wise Education and IT Tallaght"	Educational dis-advantage	Students in West Tallaght (15-19)	Dublin	Dublin (West Tallaght)	€376,800
iScoil	Educational dis-advantage	Early school leavers or those at risk of leaving school (13-18)	Dublin	Nation-wide	94,200
"PETE" Preparation for Education Training and Employment	Educational dis-advantage	People at risk of homelessness, who have experienced homelessness, and who are experiencing homelessn	Dublin	Dublin, Waterford & Limerick	€1,271,700

		ess			
Speedpak Group	Educational dis- advantage	People who are long term un- employed	Dublin	Dublin	€78,500
Trinity Access 21	Educational dis- advantage	Second level school students across DEIS schools	Dublin	Laois, Offaly, Kerry and Dublin	€2,056,700
Trinity Centre for People with Intellectual Disabilities	Educational dis- advantage	Young people with intellectual disabilities	Dublin	Nation- wide	€628,000

Animate Healthy Community Awards 2017 (9)

Project Name	Issue focus	Target Group	Location	Impact	Grant size €
BodyRight	Sexual violence/ consent education	Young people	Dublin	Nationwid e	€25,000 (€15,00 0 cash, €10,000 NFS)
Children's Grief Centre	Mental health (children)	Children experiencing bereavement or parental separation	Limerick	Limerick	€25,000 (€15,00 0 cash, €10,000 NFS)
Eat Well Live Well Age Well	Nutrition / Older people	Older people	Galway	Galway City/ County	€20,000 NFS
IBD Self- Managemen t	Physical health	People with inflammatory bowel disease	Dublin	Dublin	€25,000 (€15,00 0 cash, €10,000 NFS)
KICK (Kickboxing to Inspire & Challenge Kids)	Physical health/ antisocial behaviou r (teens)	Teenagers from disadvantage d socio- economic backgrounds	Dublin (Tallaght)	Dublin (Tallaght)	€25,000 (€15,00 0 cash, €10,000 NFS)
Mindfulness Based Stress Relief	Mental health	Stage IV metastatic cancer	Cork	Cork	€20,000 (€10,00 0 cash,

		patients			€10,000 NFS)
(MBSR) for Metastatic Cancer Patients					
Pavee Point Traveller Maternal Health Initiative	Physical & mental health	Traveller mothers	Dublin	Nationwide	€20,000 (€10,000 cash, €10,000 NFS)
Suicide Specific Treatment Track	Mental health	Homeless people	Dublin	Dublin, Kildare, Wicklow & Meath	€20,000 (€10,000 cash, €10,000 NFS)
TRTP Young Traveller's Project	Social skills/ mental health	Young Travellers	Tipperary	Tipperary	€20,000 (€10,000 cash, €10,000 NFS)

Animate 2017 (1)

Project Name	Issue focus	Target Group	Location	Impact	Grant size €
Not So Different	Social Inclusion / Unemployment	People with Autism spectrum disorder	Dublin	Dublin	€20,000 (€10,000 cash, €10,000 NFS)

REFERENCES

A

Amin, Ash, Angus Cameron, and Ray Hudson. 2002. *Placing the Social Economy*. London and New York: Routledge.

Amin, Ash. 2009. "Locating the Social Economy." In *The Social Economy – International Perspectives on Economic Solidarity*, ed. Ash Amin. London: Zed Books.

An Cosán Virtual Community College. 2006. *Love and Social Change: Reflecting on a Model of Community Education*. Dublin: An Cosán.

An Cosán Virtual Community College. 2017. http://www.ancosan.ie/ (May 1, 2017).

Anderson, Steven. 2014. *New Strategies for Social Innovation – Market-based Approaches for Helping the Poor*. New York: Columbia University Press.

AONTAS. 2011. *Sowing the Seeds of Social Change*. Dublin: AONTAS Publications.

Argyris, Chris, Robert Putnam, and Diane McLain Smith. 1985. *Action Science: Concepts, Methods and Skills for Research and Intervention*. San Francisco: Jossey-Bass.

Argyris, Chris, and Donald Schön. 1989. "Participatory Action Research and Action Science Compared: A commentary." *American Behavioural Scientist*, 32 (May):612 - 23.

Ashoka Change Makers. 2015. "Makers of More:Your Idea, Your Community, Your Action" https://www.changemakers.com/makersofmore (July 1, 2017).

Asimov, Isaac. 1951. "The Fun They Had." http://visualmemory.co.uk/daniel/funtheyhad.html (May 1, 2017).

Austin, James, Howard Stevenson, and Jane Wei-Skillern. 2006. "Social and Commercial Entrepreneurship: Same, Different, or Both?" *Entrepreneurship Theory and Practice*, 30 (1): 1-22.

B

Barnardos. 2016. "Back to School Survey." https://www.barnardos.ie/assets/files/Advocacy/2016Sch

oolCosts/BarnardosBacktoSchoolSurvey2016Factsheet.pdf (May 1, 2017).

Barry, Martin and Ralph Chapman. 2009. "Distributed small scale wind in New Zealand: Advantages, Barriers and Policy Instruments." *Energy Policy*, 37 (September):3358-3369.

Bauwens, Thomas. 2013. "What Roles for Energy Cooperatives in the Diffusion of Distributed Generation Technologies?" http://ssrn.com/abstract=2382596 or http://dx.doi.org/10.2139/ssrn.2382596 (October 10, 2017).

Beetham, Helen. 2013. '"Designing for Learning in an Uncertain Future." In *Rethinking Pedagogy for a Digital Age*, eds. Helen Beetham and Rhona Sharpe. London: Routledge.

Benkler, Yochai. 2006. *The Wealth of Networks: How Social Production Transforms Markets and Freedom*. New Haven: Yale University Press.

Bennett, J. 2006. "ECEC financing in Ireland." Presented at CSER Early Childhood Care and Education Seminar Series 1, Dublin.

BEPA. 2014. "Social Innovation: A Decade of Change". Luxembourg: Publications Office of the European Union.

Bhaskar, Roy. [1975] 1978. *A Realist Theory of Science*. 2nd ed. Brighton: Harvester Press.

Birchall, Johnston, and Lou Hammond Ketilson. 2009. *Responses to the Global Economic Crisis- Resilience of the Co-operative Business Model in Times of Crisis. International Labour Organisation- Sustainable Enterprise Programme*. Geneva: International Labour Organisation.

Bishop, Matthew and Michael Green. 2008. *Philanthrocapitalism – How the Rich Can Save the World and Why We Should Let Them*. London: AC Black.

Bolinger, Mark. 2001. *Community Wind Power Ownership Schemes in Europe and their Relevance to the United States*. Berkeley, CA: Lawrence Berkeley National Laboratory.

Boltanski, Luc and Eve Chiapello. 2005. *The New Spirit of Capitalism*. London: Verso.

Bosma, Niels, Thomas Schøtt, Siri Terjesen and Penny Kew. 2016. *Global Entrepreneurship Monitor – Social Entrepreneurship (Special Topic Report)* http://gemconsortium.org/report/49542 (July 5, 2017).

Brennan, Peter. 2014. "Preparing a Tender from a Suppliers' Perspective. Bid management services" https://www.slideserve.com/alanna/preparing-a-tender-from-a-suppliers-perspective (July 11, 2017).

Brennan, Peter. 2016. "Public Procurement in Ireland; a Critical Review" Presentation to the Public Policy Advisors Network Annual Conference, Dublin. http://www.ppan.ie/wp-content/uploads/2016/11/Procurement-A-critical-review-by-Doctor-Peter-Brennan-1.pdf (July 11, 2017).

Brouard, Francois and Sophie Larivet. 2010. "Essay of clarifications and definitions of the related concepts of social enterprise, social entrepreneur and social entrepreneurship." In *Handbook of Research on Social Entrepreneurship*, eds. Alain Fayolle and Harry Matlay. London: Edward Elgar Publishing Limited.

Borzaga, Carlo, and Alceste Santuiri. 2001. "Italy: From Traditional Co-operatives to Innovative Social Enterprises." In *The Emergence of Social Enterprise*, eds. Carlo Borzaga and Jacques Defourny. Routledge, London: 2001.

Borzaga, Carlo, Sara Depedri, and Ermanno Tortia. 2009. "The Role of Cooperative and Social Enterprises: A Multifaceted Approach for an Economic Pluralism." Euricse Working Papers, 000/09.

Borzaga, Carlo, Chiara Carini, Maurizio Carpita, and Massimo Lori. 2015. "The Relevance and Economic Sustainability of the Social Economy in Italy." Euricse Working Papers, 81/15.

Bourdieu, Pierre. 2008. *Political Interventions*. London: Verso.

Boyd, Stephen. 2002. *Partnership Working: European Social Partnership Models*. Glasgow: Scottish TUC.

Byrne, S., Skarlato, O., Fissuh, E., and Irvin, C. 2009. Building trust and goodwill in Northern Ireland and the Border Counties: the impact of economic aid on the peace process. *Irish Political Studies*, 24(3), 337-363.

C

Cabinet Office (n.d) "Essex County Council: Children at risk of going into care" https://data.gov.uk/sib_knowledge_box/essex-county-council-children-risk-going-care (October 3, 2017).

Cafferty, Siobhan, Olive McCarthy, and Carol Power. 2016. "Risk and Reward: The development of Social Enterprise within the Criminal Justice Sector in Ireland – Some policy implications." *Irish Probation Journal*, 13 (October):22-39.

Caporasa, James A., and David P. Levine. 1992. *Theories of Political Economy*. Cambridge: Cambridge University Press.

Cassells, Peter. 2015. "The Role, Value and Scale of Higher Education in Ireland". Discussion Paper for The Expert Group on Future Funding for Higher Education https://www.education.ie/en/The-Education-System/Higher-Education/Higher-Education-Role-Value-and-Scale-of-Higher-Education-in-Ireland-Discussion-Paper-1-.pdf (May 1, 2017).

Chadwick, Andrew. 2006. *Internet Politics: States, Citizens, and New Communication Technologies*. Oxford: Oxford University Press.

Chittum, Anna, and Poul Ostergaard. 2014. "How Danish communal heat planning empowers municipalities and benefits individual consumers." *Energy Policy* 74: 464-475.

Chomsky, Noam. 2004. *Hegemony or survival? America's quest for global dominance*. UK: Penguin.

Clancy, Paula and Grainne Murphy. 2006. *Outsourcing Government – Public Bodies and Accountability*. Dublin: TASC/New Island.

Coghlan, David, and Teresa Brannick. [2001] 2005. *Doing action research in your own organization*. 2nd ed. London: Sage.

Cole, George Douglas Howard. 1920. *Guild Socialism Restated*. London: Routledge.

Comhar and Trinity College Dublin. 2011. "Community Renewable Energy in Ireland: Status, Barriers and Potential Options, Policy Paper" http://files.nesc.ie.s3.amazonaws.com/nesf_archive/nesf_reports/NESF_39_full.pdf (October 3, 2017).Committee on the Future of Healthcare. 2016. "*Future of ehealth in Ireland debate*" http://beta.oireachtas.ie/en/debates/debate/committee_on_the_future_of_healthcare/2016-09-14/3/ (July 11, 2017).

Connolly, Bríd. 2001. *Women's Community Education in Ireland*. Dublin: AONTAS Publications.

Connolly, Bríd. 2003. "Community Education: Listening to the Voices" http://www.cavanadulteducation.ie/images/uploads/2003 _Community_Education_Listening2Voices.pdf (May 1, 2017).

Connolly, David, and Brian Vad Mathiesen. 2014. "A technical and economic analysis of one potential pathway to a 100% renewable energy system." *International Journal of Sustainable Energy Planning and Management* 1 (2014):7-28.

Cooke, Bill, and Uma Kothari, eds. 2001. *Participation: The New Tyranny?* London: Zed Books.

Cornia, Giovanni Andrea, Roberto De Vogli, Ritesh Mistry, and Roberto Gnesotto. 2005. "Has the relation between income inequality and life expectancy disappeared? Evidence from Italy and top industrialised countries." *Journal of Epidemiol Community Health* 59 (February) 158–162.

Corrigan, Tony, and Mangan O Beirne. 2014. "Ireland's tender process needs transparency" *The Global Legal Post* http://www.globallegalpost.com/blogs/commentary/irelan ds-tender-process-needs-transparency-82980171/ (July 11, 2017).

Colvin, Christopher and Eoin McLaughlin. 2012. "Raiffeisenism Abroad: Why Did German Microfinance fail in Ireland but Prosper in the Netherlands." European University Institute Max Weber Programme Working papers (2012/01) http://cadmus.eui.eu/bitstream/handle/1814/20314/MWP _Colvin_McLaughlin_2012_01.pdf?sequence=1&isAllowed=y (October 3, 2017).

Cosgrove, Faye, Maggie O'Neill, and John Sargent. 2011. "Can Social Enterprise Reduce Reoffending?" School of Applied Social Sciences Research Briefing No. 4. Durham, UK: Durham University https://www.dur.ac.uk/sass/research/briefings (October 3, 2017).

Craig, Ben, and John Pencavel. 1995. "Participation and productivity: A comparison of worker cooperatives and conventional firms in the plywood industry." https://www.brookings.edu/bpea-articles/participation-and-productiviy-a-comparison-of-worker-cooperatives-and-conventional-firms-in-the-plywood-industry/ (October 3, 2017).

CSO. 2016. *Census of Population 2016 – Profile 7 Migration and Diversity.*

http://www.cso.ie/en/releasesandpublications/ep/p-cp7md/p7md/p7anii/(October 3, 2017).

Curtis, Alan. 2013. "Social Enterprise and the effect of Isomorphism: The blurring boundaries between the not for profit and for profit market (Carebright Case Study)." EMES-SOCENT Conference Selected Papers, no. LG13-66 https://www.iap-socent.be/sites/default/files/Curtis%20ECSP-LG13-66.pdf (July 11, 2017).

D

Dáil Éireann Debates. 2016. Vol. 886 No. 4, 9 July 2015 http://oireachtasdebates.oireachtas.ie/debates%20authoring/debateswebpack.nsf/takes/dail2015070900006?opendocument#D00200 (July 11, 2017).

Dáil Éireann Debates. 2017. Vol. 934 No. 1, 17 January 2017 http://oireachtasdebates.oireachtas.ie/debates%20authoring/debateswebpack.nsf/takes/dail2017011700099#WRNN02500 (July 1, 2017).

Dahlberg, Gunilla, Peter Moss, and Alan Pence, eds. 1999. *Beyond Quality in Early Childhood Education and Care: Postmodern Perspectives*. London: Falmer Press.

Dees, Gregory, J. 1998. *The meaning of social entrepreneurship*. Working paper, Kauffman Center for Entrepreneurial Leadership https://entrepreneurship.duke.edu/news-item/the-meaning-of-social-entrepreneurship/(July 5, 2017).

Dees, Gregory, J., and Beth Battle Anderson, and Jane Wei-Skillern. 2002. "Pathways to Social Impact: Strategies for Scaling Out Successful Social Innovations, CASE Working Paper Series No. 3, Center for the Advancement of Social Entrepreneurship, North Carolina: Duke's Fuqua School of Business.

Defourny, Jacques and Marthe Nyssens. 2006. "Defining Social Enterprise." In *Social Enterprise - At the Crossroads of Market, Public Policies and Civil Society*, ed. Marthe Nyssens. London: Routledge.

Defourny, Jacques. 2010. "Concepts and Realities of Social Enterprise: A European Perspective." In *Handbook of Research on Social Entrepreneurship*, eds. Alain Fayolle and Harry Matlay. Cheltenham: Edward Elgar.

Defourny, Jacques and Marthe Nyssens. 2010. "Conceptions of Social Enterprise and Social Entrepreneurship in Europe and the United States: Convergences and Divergences", *Journal of Social Entrepreneurship*, Volume 1 (1): 32-53.

Defourny, Jacques and Marthe Nyssens. 2012. *The EMES approach of social enterprise in a comparative perspective*. Brussels: EMES. http://emes.net/publications/working-papers/the-emes-approach-of-social-enterprise-in-a-comparative-perspective/ (July 5, 2017).

Department of Communications, Energy and Natural Resources. 2012. *Delivering a Connected Society: a National Broadband Plan for Ireland*. http://www.dccae.gov.ie/documents/National%20Broadband%20Plan.pdf (May 1, 2017).

Department of Education and Science. 2001. *A brief description of the Irish education system*. Dublin: DES Communications Unit.

Department of Education and Skills. 2016. *Investing in National Ambition: A Strategy for Funding Higher Education*. http://www.education.ie/en/Publications/Policy-Reports/Investing-in-NationalAmbition-A-Strategy-for-Funding-Higher-Education.pdf (May 1, 2017).

Department of Justice Equality and Law Reform. 2004. *Developing childcare in Ireland: A review of progress to end June 2003 on the implementation of the Equal Opportunities Childcare Programme 2000 - 2006*. Dublin: Stationery Office.

Department of Justice and Equality. 2017. *A New Way Forward: Social Enterprise Strategy 2017 – 2019*, http://www.justice.ie/EN/PB//WebPages/WP17000016 (October 6, 2017).

Department of Health. 1953. *Health Act 1953*. Dublin: Stationery Office.

Department of Health and Children. 2004. *Health Act 2004*. Dublin: Stationery Office.

Department of Health. 2013. *eHealth Strategy for Ireland*. Dublin: Stationery Office.

Department of Health. 2012. *Value for Money and Policy Review of Disability Services in Ireland*. Dublin: Stationery Office.

Devine-Wright, Patrick. 2005. "Lower Aspects of UK Renewable Energy Development: Exploring Public Beliefs and Policy Implications", *Local Environment*, 10 (January), 57–69.

Doyle, Gerard and Tanya Lalor. 2010. *Social Enterprise – An overlooked approach to promoting sustainable economic regeneration*. Dublin: Tasc Thinkpieces.

Doyle, Gerard, and Tanya Lalor, eds. 2012. *Social Enterprise in Ireland: A People's Economy?* Cork: Oak Tree Press.

Dyer-Witherford, Nick. 2015. *Cyber-Proletariat*. London: Pluto Press.

E

Earle Joe, Cathal Moran, and Zach Ward-Perkins. 2016. *The Econocracy*, Manchester: Manchester University Press.

Easton, Geoff. 2009. "Critical realism in case study research." *Industrial Marketing Management* 39 (2010):118-28.

Edmiston, Daniel. 2015. "Social Innovation Policy in Hungary". CRESSI Working Paper Series No. 21/2015. Oxford: University of Oxford.

Edwards, Michael. 2009. "Philanthrocapitalism: after the goldrush", in Tony Curzon Price and David Hayes, eds., *The Power of Giving – Philanthrocapitalism Debated*. London: Open Democracy.

Emerson, Jed. 2003. "The Blended Value Proposition: Integrating Social and Financial Returns", *California Management Review*, vol. 45, no. 4, summer.

Erdal, David. 2000. "The Psychology of Sharing: An Evolutionary Approach". Ph.D. diss. St. Andrew's University.

Erdal, David. 2011. *Beyond the Corporation: Humanity Working*. London: Bodley Head.

Eustace, Anne. and Ann Clarke. 2009. *Exploring Social Enterprise, Final Report*, Dublin: Eustace Patterson.

European Commission Childcare Network. 1990. *Quality in Childcare Services: Report on an EC Technical Seminar*. Barcelona: ECCN.

European Commission. 1993. *Growth, Competitiveness, Employment: The Challenges and Ways Forward into the 21st*

Century - White Paper. Parts A and B. Brussels: Bulletin of the European Communities

European Commission. 2011. *Social Business Initiative - Creating a favourable climate for social enterprises, key stakeholders in the social economy and innovation.* Brussels: European Commission. http://ec.europa.eu/internal_market/social_business/docs/COM2011_682_en.pdf . (July 5, 2017).

European Commission. 2013. "Towards Social Investment for Growth and Cohesion – including implementing the European Social Fund 2014-2020" Communication from the Commission to the European Parliament, the Council, the European Economic and Social Committee and the Committee of the Regions http://eur-lex.europa.eu/LexUriServ/LexUriServ.do?uri=COM:2013:0083:FIN:en:PDF (October 3, 2017).

European Commission. 2017. *Country Report Ireland.* https://ec.europa.eu/info/sites/info/files/2017-european-semester-country-report-ireland-en.pdf (May 1, 2017).

Everett, John. 2009. *Developing and Supporting Social Enterprises in the Dublin Region: The Basis for a Comprehensive Strategy,* Dublin: Dublin Employment Pact and Clann Credo.

Eversole, Robyn, Jo Barraket and Belinda Luke. 2014. 'Social enterprises in rural community development', in *Community Development Journal,* Volume 49 (2): 245-261.

F

Fahey, Tony, Helen Russell, and Emer Smyth. 2000. "Gender equality, fertility decline and labour market patterns among women in Ireland." In *Bust to boom? The Irish experience of growth and inequality,* eds. Nolan, B., Philip J. O'Connell and Christopher T. Whelan. Dublin: IPA.

Fahey, Tony. 2007. "The Catholic Church and Social Policy", in Reynolds Brigid, and Sean Healy, eds., *Values, Catholic Social Thought and Public Policy,* 143-163, Dublin: Cori Justice.

Fanning, B. 2002. *Racism and social change in the Republic of Ireland.* Manchester: Manchester University Press.

Farrington, David. P., Geoffrey C. Barnes, and Sandra Lambert. 1996. "The concentration of offending in families", *Legal and Criminological Psychology*, vol. 1, 47–63.

Feasta. 2007. *Envisioning a Sustainable Ireland from an Availability Perspective – A Report to the Environmental Protection Agency.* Dublin: Feasta.

Feldman, A., Gilmartin, M., Loyal, S., and Migge, B. 2008. *Getting on: From migration to integration - Chinese, Indian, Lithuanian and Nigerian migrants' experiences in Ireland.* Dublin: Immigrant Council of Ireland.

Fici, Antonio. 2010. "Italian co-operative law reform and co-operative principles", Euricse Working Papers, No. 002/2010.

Fine, Ben. 2001. *Social Capital versus Social Theory.* London: Routledge.

Fleming, Bairbre. 2013. "Fish in water: Is mature student access to Irish higher education experienced equally and fairly?" In *How Equal? Access to Higher Education Research Papers.* Dublin: Higher Education Authority.

Forfás. 2013. *Social Enterprise in Ireland, Sectoral Opportunities and Policy Issues*, Dublin: Forfás.

Fougère, Martin, Beata Segercrantz and Hannele Seeck. 2017. "A critical reading of the European Union's social innovation policy discourse: (Re) legitimizing neoliberalism", *Organisation*, Volume 24 (1):1-17.Freire, Paulo. 2001. *Pedagogy of Freedom: Ethics, Democracy, and Civic Courage.* Oxford: Rowman and Littlefield.

G

Gallagher, Seán. 2000. "P. J. Meghan and approved local councils: a neglected experiment in community development", *Administration*, Volume 48(2): 77–91.

Gardner, C., Isard, P., Dermody, A., Fraser, S. and Quigley, M. 2014. *Research into Social Enterprise in South and East Cork: Supports Required to Develop the Social Enterprise Sector in the SECAD Area.* Cork: SECAD.

Government of Ireland. 2003. 'Measuring Ireland's Progress, 2003.' *Central Statistics Office Indicator Reports.* Dublin: Government Publications.

Government of Ireland. 2016. *Programme for Partnership Government*: Dublin: Government Publications Office.

Gummesson, Evert. 2000. *Qualitative methods in management research*. 2nd ed. London: Sage Publication Inc.

H

Hainsworth, P. (Ed.). 1998. *Divided society: Ethnic minorities and racism in Northern Ireland*. London: Pluto Press.

Harris, Michael and David Albury. 2009. *The Innovation Imperative*. London: NESTA.

Harvey, David. 2007. *A Brief History of Neoliberalism*. Oxford: Oxford University Press.

Harvey Juliet A., Sebastien F.M. Chastin, and Dawn A. Skelton. 2013. "Prevalence of Sedentary Behaviour in Older Adults: A Systematic Review." *International Journal of Environmental Research and Public Health* 10(12):6645-6661.

Harvey, Brian. 2013. "Travelling with Austerity". http://www.paveepoint.ie/wp-content/uploads/2013/10/Travelling-with-Austerity_Pavee-Point-2013.pdf (May 1, 2017).

Hastings, Tim, Brian Sheehan and Padraig Yeates. 2007. *Saving the Future: How Social Partnership Shaped Ireland's Economic Success*. Dublin: Blackhall Publishing.

Hayes, Noirin. 2002. "Children's rights - Whose right: a review of child policy development in Ireland." *Policy Paper*. Dublin: Policy Institute, TCD.

Hayes, Noirin and Siobhan Bradley. 2006. "Early childhood education and care: A decade of reflection 1996-2006." Paper read at CSER Early Childhood Care and Education Seminar Series 1, Dublin.

HEA. 2013. *How Equal? Access to Higher Education Research Papers*. Dublin: Higher Education Authority.

HEA. 2014. *Towards the Development of a New National Plan for Equity of Access to Higher Education*. Dublin: Higher Education Authority.

Hicks, David. 2004. "Radical Education". *Education Studies: A Student Guide*. Stephen Ward, ed. Routledge: Falmer.

Heffernan, V. 2007. *History of Our Lady's Grove*. Dublin: Our Lady's Grove Primary School.

HSE. 2016. *Performance Report August/September 2016* https://www.hse.ie/eng/services/publications/performanc ereports/august-september-2016-performance-report-.pdf (July 1, 2017).

HSE. 2016. *Building a Better Health Service; annual report and financial statements 2016* http://hse.ie/eng/services/publications/corporate/Annual -Report-and-Annual-Financial-Statements-2016.pdf (July 14, 2017).

Huybrechts, Benjamin and Sybille Mertens. 2011. "The role of social enterprises in institutionalizing social innovation: the case of renewable energy source cooperatives (REScoops) in Europe." Working Paper, HEC Management School. Belgium: University of Lieg.

Hynes, Briga. 2016. "Creating an enabling, supportive environment for the social enterprise sector in Ireland." Submission to the Irish Local Development Network https://www.pobal.ie/Publications/Documents/Social%20 Enterprises%20report%20master%20doc.pdf (July 13, 2016).

I

ICF Consulting. 2014. *A map of social enterprises and their eco- systems in Europe, country report: Ireland.* http://www.euricse.eu/projects/a-map-of-social- enterprises-and-their-eco-system-in-europe/ (July 1, 2017).

IGEES. 2015. *Social impact investments in Ireland, learning from the pilot initiative* http://igees.gov.ie/wp- content/uploads/2015/06/Social-Impact-Investments-in- Ireland-Learnings-from-the-Pilot-Initiative-FINAL-docx.pdf (July 11, 2017).

Innovate Dublin. 2017. http://www.innovatedublin.org/en/what-social- innovation?gclid=COmGxuO33NQCFZ2p7QodtJAEMg%20d ownloaded%2026/6/17 (October 6, 2017).

International Telecommunication Union. 2017. *ICT Facts and Figures.* http://www.itu.int/en/ITU- D/Statistics/Documents/facts/ICTFactsFigures2016.pdf (May 1, 2017).

Irish Penal Reform Trust. 2017. *Facts and Figures*, Dublin: IPRT. http://www.iprt.ie/prison-facts-2 (October 6, 2017).

Irish Statue Book, *Probation of Offenders Act, 1907*. http://www.irishstatutebook.ie/eli/1907/act/17/enacted/en/print.html (October 6, 2017).

J

Johnson, L., Adams Becker, S., Cummins, M., Estrada, V., and Freeman, A. 2015. *2015 NMC Technology Outlook for Higher Education in Ireland: A Horizon Project Regional Report*. Austin, Texas: The New Media Consortium.

Joint Committee on Jobs, Enterprise and Innovation. 2013. Houses of the Oireachtas Tuesday, 2 July 2013. http://oireachtasdebates.oireachtas.ie/debates%20authoring/debateswebpack.nsf/committeetakes/BUJ2013070200003 (July 11, 2017).

Jones, Jacky. 2016. 'Are Government-funded charities really doing 'great work?' *The Irish Times*, 12th July, 2016. https://www.irishtimes.com/life-and-style/health-family/are-government-funded-charities-really-doing-great-work-1.2713506 (October 6, 2017).

K

Kaderabkova, Anna and Saeed Moghadam Saman. 2013. *Evaluation of Social Innovations – Their Characteristics and Impacts, Cross-county Comparisons and Implications for Policy Support*. http://www.transitsocialinnovation.eu/content/original/Book%20covers/Local%20PDFs/101%20SF%20Kaderabkova%20and%20Saman%20Evaluation%20of%20SI%20cross%20country%20comparisons%202013.pdf (July 5, 2017).

Kirby, Peadar. 2002. *The celtic tiger in distress: Growth with inequality in Ireland*. Bassingstoke, UK: Palgrave.

Kretz, Andrew and Creso Sá. 2015. 'Students and Startups', in *The Transformation of University Institutional and Organizational Boundaries*, eds. Emanuela Reale and Emilia Primeri. Higher Education Research in the 21st Century Series. Rotterdam: Sense Publishers.

L

Lalor, Tanya. 2014. "Co-op Power: Opportunities for Community Energy Production in Ireland". Dublin: Report of a seminar hosted by the Society for Co-operative Studies in Ireland. Dublin: Society for Co-operative Studies in Ireland.

LaMarche, Gara. 2009. "Philanthropy for Social Change", in Tony Curzon Price and David Hayes, eds. *The Power of Giving – Philanthrocapitalism Debated*. London: Open Democracy.

Lappe, Francis M. 2006. "A Market Without Capitalists". *Alternet*, 23rd June, 2017 http://www.alternet.org/story/37920/ (October 6, 2017).

Larsen, Jens H.M., Hans C. Soerensen, Erik Christiansen, Stefan Naef, and Per Vølund. 2006. 'Experiences from Middelgrunden 40 MW Offshore Wind Farm.' Paper presented to Copenhagen Offshore Wind Seminar 26-28 October 2005 at Copenhagen, Denmark.

Laville, Jean-Louis. 2015. "Social and Solidarity Economy in Historical Perspective", in *Social and Solidarity Economy – Beyond the Fringe*, Peter Utting, ed. London: Zed Books.

Leinonen, Teemu, Tere Vadén, and Juha Suoranta. 2009. "Learning in and with an open wiki project". http://firstmonday.org/article/view/2252/2093 (May 1, 2017).

Lentin, R. 2006. *After optimism? Ireland, racism and globalisation*. Dublin: Metro Eireann Publications.

Lewin, Kurt. 1946. "Action research and minority problems." *Journal of Social Issues* 2 (34-46).

Lindblom, Charles. 2001. *The Market System: What It Is, How It Works and What to Make Of It*. New Haven: Yale University Press.

Llie, Elizabeth and Raul During. 2012. *An Analysis of SI discourses in Europe. Concepts and Strategies of Social Innovation*. Wageningen: Alterra.

Logue, John. 2006. "Economics, Cooperation, and Employee Ownership: The Emilia Romagna model - in more detail". http://community-wealth.org/sites/clone.community-wealth.org/files/downloads/article-logue_0.pdf (October 6, 2017).

Lynch, Kathleen. 2014. "Economic Inequality creates Educational Inequalities". *Village Magazine*, 18th February, 2014. https://villagemagazine.ie/index.php/2014/02/by-kathleen-lynch-economic-inequality-creates-educational-inequalities-and-class-based-cuts-to-education-an-engine-for-equality-subvert-other-rights-and-goods-for-the-most-vulnerable/ (October 6, 2017).

M

Maegaard, Preben. 2009. *Danish Renewable Energy Policy*. Bonn: World Council for Renewable Energy. http://wcre.de/images/stories/pdf/WCRE_Maegaard_Danish%20RE%20Policy.pdf (October 6, 2017).

Mair, George and Chris May. 1997. *Offenders on Probation*, Research Study 167, London: Home Office.

Marsh, John. 2011. *Class Dismissed: Why We Cannot Teach or Learn Our Way Out of Inequality*. New York: Monthly Review Press.

Martin, Roger and Sally Osberg. 2007. "Social Entrepreneurship: The Case for Definition." *Stanford Social Innovation Review*. Volume 7 (1). https://ssir.org/articles/entry/social_entrepreneurship_the_case_for_definition (July 5, 2017).

Marquardt, Steffen and Sean Sinico. 2009. "More German firms turn to cooperatives in tough economic times", *Deutsche Welle*, 13th April 2009. http://www.dw.com/en/more-german-firms-turn-to-cooperatives-in-tough-economic-times/a-4159826.

Maruna, Shadd. 1997. "Desistance and development: The psychosocial process of "going straight", *The British Criminology Conference: Selected Proceedings*, vol. 2.

Mason, Paul. 2015. *Postcapitalism*. London: Allen Lane.

McDermott, P. 2011. *Migrant languages in the public space: A case study from Northern Ireland*. LIT Verlag Münster

McDermott, P. 2015. *Attitudes towards minority ethnic people and migrant workers 2014. ARK Research Update, 103*

McGuinness, Seamus, Adele Bergin, and Adele Whelan. 2016. "An Exploration of (Area-based) Social Inclusion and Community Development Training Programmes in Ireland", ESRI Research Series No. 54. Dublin: ESRI.

McInerney, Chris, and Cian Finn. 2015. *Caring – at what cost? Rebuilding and refinancing the community and voluntary sector.* Dublin: IMPACT.

McKee, R. 2016. "Love thy neighbour? Exploring prejudice against ethnic minority groups in a divided society: the case of Northern Ireland". *Journal of Ethnic and Migration Studies,* 42(5), 777-796.

McNeill, Fergus, Stephen Farrall, Claire Lightowler, and Shadd Maruna. 2013. "How and why people stop offending: Discovering desistance", *IRISS Insights,* no. 15. https://www.iriss.org.uk/resources/insights/how-why-people-stop-offending-discovering-desistance (October 6, 2017).

Meijvogel, R., and P. Petrie. 1996. *School age childcare in the European Union.* Network on Childcare and Other Measures to Reconcile Employment and Family Responsibilities, Brussels: European Commission.

Mendonc, Miguel, Stephen Lacey, and Frede Hvelplund. 2009. "Stability, participation and transparency in renewable energy policy: Lessons from Denmark and the United States." *Policy and Society,* 27:379–398.

Migge, B. and Gilmartin, M. 2011. "Migrants and healthcare: investigating patient mobility among migrants in Ireland." *Health and Place,* 17(5):1144-1149.

Miller, Ethan. 2006. "Our eyes on the prize: From a 'worker coop movement' to a transformative social movement." *Grassroots Economic Organizing,* Newsletter, 72/73. http://www.geo.coop/node/197 (October 6, 2017).

Mintz, S. 2008. "Food and diaspora." *Food, Culture & Society,* 11(4):509-523.

Mjoset, Lars. 1992. *The Irish economy in a comparative institutional perspective.* Dublin NESC.

Monzón, José Luis and Rafael Chaves. 2012. *The Social Economy in the European Union.* Brussels: European Economic and Social Committee.

Morgan, Glenn. 2004. "Changing Capitalisms?", in Glenn Morgan, Richard Whitley and Eli Moen, eds. *Changing Capitalisms? Internationalization, institutional Change and Systems of Economic Organization.* Oxford: Oxford University Press.

Moses, Paul. 2010. "Course Correction", *Commonweal* Volume 137 (16):34-36.

Moss, Peter. 2001. "Beyond early childhood education and care." Paper read at Early Childhood Education and Care, 13-15 June, 2001, at Stockholm.

Mulgan Geoff. 2006. "The Process of Social Innovation." *Innovations*, 1:145-162.

Mulgan, Geoff. 2007. *Social Innovation: what it is, why it matters, how it can be accelerated.* Oxford: Said Business School.

Murray, Robin, Julie Caulier-Grice, and Geoff Mulgan. 2010. *The Open Book of Social Innovation.* London: The Young Foundation and NESTA.

Murray, Thomas. 2016. *Contesting Economic and Social Rights in Ireland. Constitution, State and Society, 1848-2016.* Cambridge: Cambridge University Press.

N

Nicholls, Alex. 2008. *Social Entrepreneurship – New Models of Sustainable Change.* Oxford: Oxford University Press.

NISRA 2011. *Northern Ireland Census,* 2011. Belfast: NISRA.

Núñez, G. and Heyman, J. 2007. "Entrapment processes and immigrant communities in a time of heightened border vigilance." *Human Organization,* 66(4):354-365.

Norris, Pippa. 2001. *Digital Divide: Civic Engagement, Information Poverty, and the Internet Worldwide.* Cambridge: Cambridge University Press.

Noya, Antonella and Emma Clarence. 2007. *The Social Economy: Building Inclusive Economies.* Paris: OECD

O

Ó Broin, Deiric and Eugene Waters. 2007. *Governing Below the Centre: Local Governance in Ireland.* Dublin: TASC/New Island.

Ó Broin, Deiric. 2009. "Institutionalising Social Partnership in Ireland", in *Power, Dissent and democracy – Civil Society and the State in Ireland* Deiric Ó Broin and Peadar Kirby, eds. Dublin: A and A Farmar.

Ó Broin, Deiric. 2014. 'Building Inclusive Economies: The Social Economy and Public Policy in an Era of Austerity', in

Innovation in the Social Economy – Emerging Best Practice in Ireland and Wales, Deiric Ó Broin and Peadar Kirby, eds. Dublin: Glasnevin Press.

Ó Broin, Deiric. 2015. "Politico-Cultural Change and Institutional Redsign ", in *Adapting to Climate Change: Governance Challenges,* Deiric Ó Broin and Peadar Kirby, eds. Dublin: Glasnevin Press.

O'Donnell, Rory. 1998. "Social policy in Ireland: Principles and interpretations", in *Negotiated economic and social governance and european integration,* eds. O'Donnell, Rory and Joe Larraghy. Brussels: European Community.

O'Donnell, Rory. 2000. "The new Ireland in the new Europe" in *Europe: The Irish experience,* Rory O'Donnell, ed. Dublin: IPA.

O'Donnell, Rory. 2001. "The future of social partnership in Ireland: A Discussion Paper Prepared for the National Competitiveness Council". Dublin: National Competitiveness Council.

OECD. 2001. "Starting Strong: Early childhood education and care". Paris: OECD.

OECD. 2006. "Starting Strong II: Early childhood education and care". Paris: OECD.

OECD. 2015. *Social impact investment: building the evidence base.* Paris: OECD Publishing.

OECD. 2013. *Policy Brief on Social Entrepreneurship – Entrepreneurial Activities in Europe.* Paris: OECD. https://www.oecd.org/cfe/leed/Social%20entrepreneurship%20policy%20brief%20EN_FINAL.pdf (July 6, 2017).

O'Shaughnessy, Mary, and Patricia O'Hara. 2016. "Social Enterprise in Ireland – Why Work Integration Social Enterprises (WISEs) Dominate the Discourse". *Nonprof Pol Forum 2016;* 7(4): 461–485.

O'Sullivan, Michele. 2002. "Parental involvement and participation: From rhetoric to reality in primary education." Master's Thesis, Dublin Institute of Technology: Dublin.

P

Pearce, John. 1993. *At the Heart of the Community Economy: Community Enterprise in a Changing World.* London: Calouste Gulbenkien Foundation.

Pearce, John. 1999. *Social Enterprise in Anytown*. London: Calouste Gulbenkien Foundation.

Pearce, John. 2009. "Social economy: Engaging as a Third System." In *The Social Economy: International Perspectives on Economic Solidarity*, Amin, Ash (ed.). London: Zed Books.

Perrini, Francesco. 2006. *The New Social Entrepreneurship - What Awaits Social Entrepreneurial Ventures?* Cheltenham: Edward Elgar.

Phills, James, Kriss Deiglmeier and Dale T. Miller. 2003. "Editors Note". *Stanford Social Innovation Review*, Volume 1 (1):1.

Phills, James, Kriss Deiglmeier and Dale T. Miller. 2008. 'Rediscovering Social Innovation', in *Stanford Social Innovation Review*, Volume 5 (3): 1.

Polanyi, Ken. 2001. *The Great Transformation*. Boston: Free Press.

Putnam, Robert. 2000. *Bowling Alone*. New York: Simon & Schuster.

Puttnam, David. 2015. '21st Century Learning'. https://www.youtube.com/watch?v=jw9aa1AjNKY (May 1, 2017).

R

Ranis, P. 2006. "Factories without bosses: Argentina's experience with worker run enterprises." *Labor Studies in Working Class History of the Americas*. 3(1):11-23.

Ranis, P. 2010. "Argentine worker cooperatives in civil society: a challenge to capital-labor relations," *Working USA: the Journal of Labor and Society*, 13:77-105

Ranis, P. 2016. *Cooperatives Confront Capitalism: Challenging the Neo-Liberal Economy*. London: Zed Books.

Ravitch, Diane. 2010. *The Death and Life of the Great American School System – How Testing and Choice are Undermining Education*. New York: Basic Books.

Raworth, Kate. 2017. *Doughnut Economics: Seven Ways to Think Like a 21st-Century Economist*. US: Chelsea Green Publishing Company

Reason, P, and Bradbury, H., eds. 2001. *Handbook of action research: Participative inquiry and practice*. Thousand Oaks, CA: Sage.

Restakis, John. 2005. "The Lessons of Emilia Romagna." British Columbia Co-operative Association.

Restakis, John. 2006. *Defining the Social Economy - The BC Context.* Vancouver: British Columbia Co-operative Association. Available at: http://www.msvu.ca/socialeconomyatlantic/pdfs/Defining SocialEconomy_FnlJan1906.pdf . Accessed 5th July 2017.

Restakis, John. 2007. "The Emilian Model- Profile of a Co-operative Economy. Retrieved from Athabasca University: http://auspace.athabascau.ca:8080/dspace/bitstream/2149/1111/1/Emilia_Romagna_Mod el.pdf

Restakis, John. 2010. *Humanising the Economy: Co-operatives in the Age of Capital.* Gabriola Island, BC: New Society Publishers.

Ridley-Duff, Rory and Cliff Southcombe. 2012. "The Social Enterprise Mark: a critical review of its conceptual dimensions". *Social Enterprise Journal,* Volume 8(3):178-200.

Ridley-Duff, Rory and Mike Bull. 2016. *Understanding Social Enterprise – Theory and Practice.* London: Sage.

Rinehart, J. 2009. "Building Resilient Sustainable Economies via the Cooperative Sector and Flexible Specialization: Lessons from the Emilia Romagna Region of Italy". Paper presented at conference Appalachian State University, 2nd May, 2009.

Rogers, J. C., Simmons, E.A., Convery, I., and Weatherall, A. 2008. "Public Perceptions of Opportunities for Community-based Renewable Energy Projects" *Energy Policy,* 36(11): 4217–4226.

Rorty, R. 1996. "Remarks on deconstruction and pragmatism." In *Deconstruction and pragmatism,* ed. C. Mouffe. London: Routledge.

Russon Gilman, Holly. 2016. *Democracy Reinvented.* US: Brookings Institution Press.

Ryan, Howard. 2016. *Educational Justice: Teaching and Organising against the Corporate Juggernaut.* New York: Monthly Review Press.

S

Sá, Creso and Andrew Kretz. 2015. *The Entrepreneurship Movement and the University.* New York: Palgrave Macmillan.

Sahakian, Marlyne and Christophe Dunand. 2015. "The social and solidarity economy towards greater 'sustainability': learning across contexts and cultures, from Geneva to Manila" *Community Development Journal*, Volume 50(3):403-417.

Sayer, Andrew. 2000. "Equality and Moral Economy", paper delivered at the Equality Studies Centre 10th Anniversary Conference, University college Dublin, December 15th 2000. http://www.lancs.ac.uk/fass/sociology/papers/sayer-equality-and-moral-economy.pdf (2nd July, 2012).

Seanad Éireann Debate.2013. *HSE Funding* Seanad debates Tuesday, 26 November 2013 https://www.kildarestreet.com/sendebates/?id=2013-11-26a.198 (14 July, 2017).

Seelos, Christian, and Mair, Johanna. 2016 "When Innovation Goes Wrong" *Stanford Social Innovation Review*, Vol 13(4).

Smyth, Emer, and McCoy, Selina. 2009. *Investing in Education: Combatting Educational Disadvantage*. Economic and Social Research Institute Research Series No 6. https://www.esri.ie/pubs/RS006.pdf (1 May, 2017).

Social Exclusion Unit. 2002. *Reducing Reoffending by Ex-prisoners*, Report by the Social Exclusion Unit, London: Office of the Deputy Prime Minister.

Spring, Joel. 2008. "Research on Globalization and Education" *Review of Educational Research*. 78:2 (June): 330-363.

Steinerowski, Artur and Izabella Steinerowska-Streb. 2012. "Can social enterprise contribute to creating sustainable rural communities? Using the lens of structuration theory to analyse the emergence of rural social enterprise" *Local Economy*, Volume 27(2):167-182.

Sustainable Energy Authority of Ireland (SEAI). 2010. *Renewable Energy in Ireland: Update*. Dublin: Sustainable Energy Authority of Ireland.

T

TEPSIE. 2013. "The value and role of citizen engagement in social innovation" <www.tepsie.eu>

TEPSIE. 2014. "Social Innovation. What it Is, Why it Matters and How can it be Accelerated <eureka.sbs.ox.ac.uk/761/1/social_innovation.pdf>

Thompson, J. L. 1997. *Really Useful Knowledge: Linking Theory and Practice Radical Learning for Liberation.* Connolly, B., Fleming, T., McCormack, D., and Ryan, A. eds. Maynooth: MACE.

Thyssen, M. 2016. *Keynote speech at the International Conference on Social Economy under the auspices of the Slovak Presidency of the EU Council, Bratislava.* [online] https://ec.europa.eu/commission/commissioners/2014-2019/thyssen/announcements/keynote-speech-international-conference-social-economy-under-auspices-slovak-presidency-eu-council_en [accessed 2 July 2017].

The Economist Intelligence Unit. 2016. *Social Innovation Index 2016* .http://www.eiuperspectives.economist.com/technology-innovation/old-problems-new-solutions-measuring-capacity-social-innovation-across-world-0. (7 November, 2017).

The Economist. 2010. "Let's Hear Those Ideas – A Social Innovation Briefing", August 14 2010.

The King's Fund. 2015. "Mental health under pressure". The King's Fund [online] https://www.kingsfund.org.uk/publications/mental-health-under-pressure (accessed 11 July, 2017).

The Worker Institute. 2015. *Power to the People: Toward Democratic Control of Electricity Generation.* New York: Trade Unions for Energy Democracy, Rosa Luxumberg Stiftung.

The Young Foundation. 2012. *Social Innovation Overview: A deliverable of the project: "The theoretical, empirical and policy foundations for building social innovation in Europe"* (TEPSIE), European Commission – 7th Framework Programme, Brussels: European Commission.

The Young Foundation. 2016. "Making Waves. Amplifying the potential of cities and regions through movement- based social innovation" <youngfoundation.org>

Tripodi, S., Kim, J.S. and Bender, K. 2010. *Is Employment Associated with Reduced Recidivism? The Complex Relationship between Employment and Crime,* Tallahassee: Florida State University Libraries.

199

U

Unger, Roberto Manabeira. 2009. *The Left Alternative*. London: Verso.

UNRISD. 2012. Potential and Limits of Social and Solidarity Economy. Available at: http://www.unrisd.org/sse (5 July, 2017).

Urban, M. 2006. "Strategies for change: Reflections from a systematic, comparative research project." In *CSER Early Childhood Care and Education Seminar Series 1*, N. Hayes and S. Bradley eds. Dublin: CSER.

Utting, Peter. 2015. 'The Challenge of Scaling Up Social and Solidarity Economy', in *Social and Solidarity Economy – Beyond the Fringe*. Peter Utting ed. London: Zed Books.

Uyarra, E and Flanagan, K. 2009. "Understanding the innovative impact of public procurement", Manchester Business School Working Paper No 574.

V

Visher, C.A., Winterfield, L. and Coggeshall, M.B. 2005. "Ex-offender employment programs and recidivism: A meta-analysis" *Journal of Experimental Criminology*, vol. 1:295–315.

W

Walker, B., and Salt, D. 2006. *Resilience Thinking*. Washington: Island Press.

Walker, G., Hunter S., Devine-Wright, P., Evans, R., and Fay, H. 2007. "Harnessing Community Energies: Explaining and Evaluating Community-Based Localism in Renewable Energy Policy in the UK", *Global Environmental Politics*, 7:2: 64–82.

Westall, Andrea. 2007. *How can innovation in social enterprise be understood, encouraged and enabled* London: Office of the Third Sector. Available at: https://pdfs.semanticscholar.org/f62b/29e3bbac3c0617d7f6f91679298790cf4e61.pdf . (6 July, 2017).

Wilkinson, Richard and Kate Pickett. 2009. *The Spirit Level – Why Equality is Better for Everyone*. London: Penguin.

Wonders, N. 2006. "Global flows, semi-permeable borders and new channels of inequality. Borders, mobility and technologies of control", in Pickering, S. and Weber, L. eds., *Borders, Mobility and Technologies of Control*. Dordrecht: Springer, 63-86.

Wood, Geoffrey and Ian Roper. 2004. "Towards a Revitalisation of the Public", in Pauline Dibben, Geoffrey Wood and Ian Roper eds., *Contesting Public Sector Reforms – Critical Perspectives, International Debates*. Basingstoke: Palgrave Macmillan.

WRC Social and Economic Consultants. 2003. *Evaluation of the Social Economy Programme*. Dublin: WRC Social and Economic Consultants.

Wright, Erik Olin. 2010. *Envisioning Real Utopias*. London: Verso.

Wright, Erik Olin. 2013. "Transforming Capitalism through Real Utopias" *American Sociological Review*, Volume 78 (1):1-25.

Z

Zamagni, V., and Zamagni, S,. 2010. *Cooperative enterprise: facing the challenge of globalization*. Cheltenham: Elgar.

Zografos, Christos. 2007. "Rurality discourses and the role of the social enterprise in regenerating rural Scotland" *Journal of Rural Studies*, Volume 23 (1):38-51.

Lightning Source UK Ltd.
Milton Keynes UK
UKOW04f2326221117

313134UK00001B/101/P